COLD
MOUNTAIN

Charles Frazier

TECHNICAL DIRECTOR Maxwell Krohn
EDITORIAL DIRECTOR Justin Kestler
MANAGING EDITOR Ben Florman

SERIES EDITORS Boomie Aglietti, Justin Kestler
PRODUCTION Christian Lorentzen

WRITER Catherine Buchanan
EDITORS Benjamin Morgan, Dennis Quinio

This edition published by Spark Publishing

Spark Publishing
A Division of SparkNotes LLC
120 Fifth Avenue, 8th Floor
New York, NY 10011

02 03 04 05 SN 9 8 7 6 5 4 3 2 1

Please send all comments and questions or report errors to
feedback@sparknotes.com.

Library of Congress information available upon request

Printed and bound in the United States

RRD-C

ISBN 1-58663-505-0

Introduction:
Stopping to Buy Sparknotes on a Snowy Evening

Whose words these are you *think* you know.
Your paper's due tomorrow, though;
We're glad to see you stopping here
To get some help before you go.

Lost your course? You'll find it here.
Face tests and essays without fear.
Between the words, good grades at stake:
Get great results throughout the year.

Once school bells caused your heart to quake
As teachers circled each mistake.
Use SparkNotes and no longer weep,
Ace every single test you take.

Yes, books are lovely, dark, and deep,
But only what you grasp you keep,
With hours to go before you sleep,
With hours to go before you sleep.

CONTENTS

Context

COLD MOUNTAIN, Charles Frazier's debut novel, won critical acclaim and the National Book Award for fiction when it was published in 1997. As an author of travel books and short stories, Frazier had ample experience in writing about landscapes and using a condensed prose style. Frazier applied these literary skills in crafting *Cold Mountain*'s episodic structure and detailed descriptive passages. Frazier's prose draws on the transcendentalism of Ralph Waldo Emerson, the scope of southern novels by authors such as William Faulkner, and the appreciation of nature expressed in the poetry of Walt Whitman. Frazier lives in North Carolina, and his choice of *Cold Mountain*'s setting along the Blue Ridge Mountains conveys his profound identification with this hallowed terrain.

The epic novel charts its course through the troubled waters of nineteenth-century American history. The action is set in 1864, three years after the outbreak of the Civil War, in an era of discord between North and South. Although the war is essentially a backdrop for events, it is clear that Inman's experiences as a Confederate soldier have profoundly affected his understanding of the world and have resurrected his dormant spiritual anxieties. Many characters tell tales of hardship and despair, some of which are war stories. These tales help develop the themes of displacement and exile that define the novel.

Frazier suggests that the war damaged Southerners both personally and politically. Frazier's characters are rarely supportive of one side or another. After three years of conflict, many are disillusioned with what they consider to be the selfish motivations of both sides. In particular, the inhabitants of Cold Mountain are presented as guarded, insular, and narrow-minded.

Frazier examines the issue of slavery in the context of the war, but as a backdrop to central events. The characters are racially diverse, but the novel tends to focus on white society. Frazier incorporates the cruel treatment meted out to slaves by Southern landowners into more general themes like human suffering and hope for a better future. Frazier is more interested in Inman and Ada's relationship to each other and to the landscape than he is in the politics of the era, leaving us to decide whether he shortchanges historical events. The novel is most effective in capturing the spirit of two people searching for self-knowledge and romantic fulfillment.

The book is also effective in presenting a view of nineteenth-century Americans' relationship to the land. Inman's obsessive drive westward is an expression of his freedom of spirit. When he is forced to retrace his steps east by the military, Inman feels as though life is slipping away from him. As Henry David Thoreau wrote in his essay "Walking," (1862), "The future lies [west] to me. . . . Eastward I go by force; but westward I go free." Frazier's novel is set on the verge of a new era, and Inman seems to symbolize the independence of spirit and dynamic will of those who will later lay claim to the West.

Although he touches upon the issue of migration westward as well as the trauma of Civil War experiences, Frazier refrains from coming to any definitive political conclusions in his novel. Instead, *Cold Mountain* examines the evolution of human relationships in tandem with the seasonal changes and variations of the natural world. Although set in the Civil War era, Frazier's work deals primarily with the timeless search for self-realization.

Plot Overview

Cold Mountain opens with its protagonist, Inman, lying in a Virginia hospital recovering from war wounds. He is shattered by the violence he has witnessed while fighting in the Confederate army and wants to go home to reunite with Ada, the woman he loves. Inman talks to a blind man and realizes that losing something you already have is worse than not getting what you want. One day in town, Inman writes to inform Ada that he is returning home. That night, he leaves the hospital through a window and sets out on his journey back to North Carolina.

The story of Inman's adventures intertwines with Ada's story. Ada is left alone to manage Black Cove Farm following her father's death. She is bereft and has no idea where she belongs or how she should earn a living. When she visits the Swangers, her neighbors, Ada looks into a well to foretell her future. She sees a man walking through the woods on a journey but does not know what this vision means. The next day, Sally Swanger sends a local girl named Ruby to help out on the farm. Ruby and Ada become friends and establish a comfortable domestic routine.

Meanwhile, Inman's journey westward is fraught with danger and violence. He is pursued across the Cape Fear River, escaping with his life thanks to the skill of a girl paddling a dugout canoe. Inman intervenes when he finds a dissolute preacher, Solomon Veasey, attempting to murder his (the preacher's) pregnant lover. The preacher is exiled from his community, and Inman is forced to continue part of his journey with Veasey. Inman has to intervene again when Veasey causes trouble in a store and at an inn. While Veasey spends the night with a prostitute called Big Tildy, the peddler Odell tells Inman a sad story about landowners' cruelty towards slaves.

The next day, Inman and Veasey help a man remove a dead bull from his stream. This man, Junior, invites them to his home to spend the night, and several strange things happen. Inman is drugged and forced to marry Junior's wife, who the author suggests may be a cannibal. Junior then hands Inman and Veasey over to the Home Guard, the military force that has been searching for Inman. Inman is forced to walk eastward, retracing his steps. The guards decide to shoot the men and bury them in a shallow grave. Although Inman escapes with a slight head wound, Veasey dies.

Ada's story resumes. The novel follows her adjustment to a life of labor in harmony with nature. Ada's friendship with Ruby blossoms as she begins to identify with the natural world. The female protagonist lays down roots at the farm and recalls memories of Inman and her father. Occasionally, she finds herself touched by events surrounding the war. A group of pilgrims forced into exile by Federal soldiers seeks shelter for a day at the farm. Ada recalls Blount, a soldier she met at a party in Charleston who later died in battle.

Finally, when Ada and Ruby visit the town of Cold Mountain, they hear a story told by a prisoner jailed for desertion. The captive tells of the sadistic Teague's band of the Home Guard. On their walk home, the two women observe some herons, and Ruby explains that a heron fathered her. Ada tells the intricate story of her parents' relationship and her mother's tragic death in childbirth. Ruby's father, Stobrod, appears later, caught in a trap the women have laid to catch a corn thief. He explains that he is living in a mountain cave with a community of outliers who object to the war. Stobrod plays his fiddle to prove that he is a changed man, but Ruby remains skeptical.

Inman's story continues. Having been dragged from the shallow grave by wild hogs, Inman meets a kind slave who feeds and clothes him and draws a map of what lies ahead. He returns to Junior's house and kills him. Inman then continues on his journey, full of despair, a "traveling shade." Inman meets an old woman who offers him shelter at her camp in the mountains. He rests and regains his strength while the woman nurses his wounds and talks about her life. Inman learns that the woman ran away from a loveless marriage and raises goats for company and sustenance. Inman identifies with the goat-woman, but concludes that he could not live such an isolated life.

Inman continues to wander and meets a man called "Potts," who directs him to a cabin belonging to Sara, a kind young woman whose husband died in battle. Sara feeds Inman, mends his clothes and tells her story. Despite her bravery, she is close to despair. The next day, Inman kills three Federal soldiers, called "Federals" in the novel, after these men threaten Sara and her baby and steal the family hog, the only form of sustenance that the family has.

At home, Ada and Ruby start harvesting apples as autumn nears. Stobrod reappears with a slow-witted banjo player named Pangle. Ruby's father asks for shelter at the farm and for food provisions, explaining that the men intend to leave the outliers' cave because it is getting too dangerous. To Ruby's annoyance, Ada agrees to help Stobrod. The men go off into the mountains with a boy from Georgia to find their own camp. Teague's Home Guard appears looking for the mountain cave and shoots Stobrod and Pangle. The Georgia boy, who survived because he hid in a thicket, runs to the farm and tells the women what happened. Ada and Ruby leave to bury the bodies and camp out in the mountains. The next day, they bury Pangle but discover that Stobrod is still alive. Ruby removes the bullet from her father and takes him to an abandoned Cherokee village.

Meanwhile, Inman reaches Black Cove Farm and finds himself in sight of Cold Mountain. The Georgia boy tells him that the women have left to bury Ruby's father. Inman climbs the mountain and finds Pangle's grave but loses Ada's tracks in the snow. The next day he hears a gunshot and finds Ada hunting turkeys. The lovers spend four days together at the Cherokee village, discussing their feelings, past experiences, and plans for the future. They decide that Inman will walk north and surrender to the Federals, since the war will be over soon. On the fifth day, Stobrod is strong enough to travel. Ada and Ruby leave for the farm and the men follow.

On the journey back to Black Cove, the Home Guard ambushes Inman and Stobrod. Inman kills all the men except for Birch, Teague's second-in-command. Birch seems powerless and scared, but he shoots Inman before the Inman can attack him. Ada hears the shots, finds Stobrod, and races back to locate Inman. She holds him in her lap as he dies.

In a brief epilogue set ten years later, Ada, her nine year-old daughter (presumably by Inman), and Ruby's family gather in the evening. Ruby has married the boy from Georgia, called Reid, and has had three sons with him. The family sits down to eat. When the meal is over, Stobrod plays his fiddle and Ada reads to the children.

CHARACTER LIST

Inman   The male protagonist. The novel follows Inman's journey home from the slaughter he has witnessed in the Civil War. Inman is intelligent, literate, and sensitive, although he often appears emotionally reserved. Troubled by the carnage he has witnessed, Inman seeks spiritual solace in the natural world and in his memories of Ada. He attempts to retain his hope and his faith in a better world in the face of incomprehensible violence and cruelty.

Ada Monroe The female protagonist and Inman's lover. Roughly half of the novel is written from her perspective. Ada is a highly educated, literate, and intensely private young woman. The novel begins six years after she moves with her father from Charleston to Cold Mountain. She has experienced the hardship and loss of her father's death, and she has been left penniless and in charge of the farm. Ada feels alienated from small town society and rejects its restrictive mentality.

Ruby Thewes To an extent, Ruby is a foil to Ada. Uneducated and illiterate, Ruby possesses a store of knowledge about the natural world that she gleaned while younger, when her father would leave her for weeks at a time to go drinking. Ruby speaks plainly and insists on being treated like an equal. She possesses a warm and loyal heart underneath her gruff exterior. She supports her father when he returns as an army deserter to seek her help.

Monroe   Ada's dead father and the old preacher of Cold Mountain. Monroe moved with his daughter to Black Cove to speed his recovery from consumption. His wife died giving birth their daughter. A kind man and unconventional preacher, Monroe recognizes in hindsight that he has been overly protective of Ada.

Stobrod Thewes Ruby's father. Despite his drunk and disreputable past, Stobrod partially redeems himself through music. He delights in composing and performing his own fiddle tunes. As an outlier living in a cave on Cold Mountain, Stobrod looks to his daughter for help in evading the Home Guard. Even when down on his luck, Stobrod always manages to pull through, as evidenced by his narrow brush with death at the hands of Teague's men.

Solomon Veasey A preacher whom Inman exposes for trying to murder his pregnant lover. Veasey reunites with Inman on his journey west, proving to be an unintentionally dangerous, though humorous, traveling companion. As he uses religion to justify his immoral acts, Veasey symbolizes both the hypocrisy of false faith and unrestrained selfishness.

Pangle A fellow outlier and friend of Stobrod's. Though simple-minded, Pangle possesses a talent for playing the banjo and teams up with Stobrod to form a musical duo. Pangle's death stands as a testament to man's heartlessness in times of war and to wasted human life.

The goat-woman A woman who lives in the mountains and raises goats, whom Inman encounters on his journey. The goat-woman possesses a strong connection to the natural world, healing Inman's wounds with the help of food and medicine. Frazier uses her character to highlight the advantages and the disadvantages of a reclusive life (advantages and disadvantages which Inman ponders throughout his journey). Although the goat-woman finds her solace in nature, Inman realizes that she has sacrificed a deeper human relationship in order to do so.

Teague The leader of a band of the Home Guard, a local militia charged with rounding up the deserters. Teague is a cunning sadist who is mentioned by both the Ada's neighbors, the Swangers, and the captive with fear and disgust. He represents the assumed authority of the army whose crimes are justified in the name of war. His execution of Pangle and other outliers in the text foreshadows Inman's death at the hands of Birch.

Birch   Teague's young associate who kills Inman. Although Birch convinces Teague to bring the captive into town instead of hanging him, he is not a sympathetic figure. With his white hair and glassy eyes, the boy appears deadened by the violence he has witnessed.

Junior   Junior befriends Inman and Veasey before handing them over to the Home Guard. Inman's unsettling experiences at Junior's home suggest the character may be a murderer who feeds his family human flesh.

Odell   A peddler who meets Inman at an inn and tells him the sad tale of his lifelong search for Lucinda, the slave-girl that he loves. Odell's story parallels Inman's own quest to return to Ada and acts as a reminder that the Southern army was fighting in part to uphold the legality of slavery.

The captive   A deserter awaiting execution whose tale Ada and Ruby overhear one day in town. The man tells of his experiences at the hands of Teague's band of Home Guard, who shot his father for harboring outliers. The captive insists that the world is about to end because of the evil perpetrated in the name of war. The prisoner is the only character to speak out against the war because he has nothing left to lose.

The Swangers   Ada's closest neighbors and friends. The Swangers oppose the war, although both their sons are off fighting. Deeply religious, the couple was offended by Monroe's assumptions when he first arrived at Cold Mountain that they did not know the Bible. In an important, neighborly gesture, Sally sends Ruby to help out at the farm after realizing that Ada intends to run it herself. The Swangers possess the quiet endurance that characterizes many people in the novel.

Sara　　An eighteen-year-old widow who offers Inman food and shelter. Inman feels bound to help when Federal soldiers steal her hog, the only thing she and her baby have to live on. Her husband died in battle, and she characterizes the resilience of many people in the novel whose lives have been blighted by the war.

The Georgia boy A young man who sets out with Stobrod and Pangle to found a community of outliers at Shining Rocks. He avoids getting shot by Teague by hiding in a thicket, and he later marries Ruby.

Swimmer　A Cherokee boy Inman met in his youth. Inman recalls Swimmer's tales about gateways to an invisible spirit world found atop high mountains.

Big Tildy　The prostitute Veasey spends a night with at the inn. Big Tildy is strong and seems capable of overpowering most men. As a black woman who is not a slave, she does not conform to social conventions.

Laura Foster The girl Veasey attempts to murder because she is pregnant with his baby.

Blount　　A man Ada met at the last party she attended in Charleston.

Mrs. McKennet A friend of Monroe's who lives in Cold Mountain town.

The yellow man The kind slave who gives Inman food and shelter after he gets shot by the Home Guard.

Waldo　　Ada's cow.

Ralph　　Ada's horse.

ANALYSIS OF MAJOR CHARACTERS

INMAN

Inman's character reflects a conflict between moral precepts and the horrific realities of life. When the novel opens, Inman is wounded and psychologically scarred by memories of war. The ghosts of dead soldiers haunt his dreams at night and thoughts of Ada fill his days. Despite his crippled psyche, Inman remains an honorable and heroic man. Throughout the novel, Inman's conscience guides his actions. Although he is troubled by the deaths he has witnessed and doesn't wish to add to them, Inman is willing to resort to violence if necessary. Frazier characterizes his protagonist as a warrior equipped to fight moral and physical battles.

As a figure assaulted by evil forces, Inman justifies aggressive means in the name of protecting innocent people, himself included. Consequently, Inman's journey is ideological as well as geographical. Inman reconsiders his spiritual ideas in light of the physical danger and suffering he encounters while traveling. Inman's travel book, Bartram's *Travels,* is a spiritual and topographical guide—it inspires Inman with idealized visions of home and directs him towards that home. Inman consults the book for spiritual sustenance and for escapist entertainment. Frazier fills Inman's journey with shades of deeper meaning, suggesting that his physical travails mirror a more profound spiritual struggle.

Inman recalls and reinterprets past events as part of his process of spiritual awakening. In particular, he remembers Cherokee folktales and envisions a world located beyond the terrestrial realm. Inman needs this kind of comfort, for, as he delves deeper into the mountains, he becomes better acquainted with man's capacity for both good and evil. Following his encounters with Junior and his near-death experience, Inman's faith in himself falters. However, his faith in a better world does not. Frazier suggests that Sara's and the goat-woman's bravery also bolster Inman's resolve. Inman preserves his humanity under the weight of intense psychological strain because he believes in a distant and better reality.

Inman's name (we never learn his first name) suggests that he is a self-reflective man, alone in the thrall of forces greater than his own will. Inman cannot direct what happens to him, so he seeks a measure of control by inwardly questioning his past and speculating about his future. While it would be too simplistic to state that Inman finds himself in Ada, he clearly identifies in her the kind of life he wants to live—a life of peace, stability, and affection. Thus Inman grows from a tortured and disillusioned man into a calmer, more self-aware individual. Indeed, after a journey fraught with suffering and spiritual turmoil, Inman is temporarily redeemed by love. Ultimately, however, Frazier suggests that Inman's true redemption—an escape from the world with which he has become so disillusioned—can only be attained through death.

ADA

During the course of this novel, Ada's character matures dramatically. Critical of the self-interest displayed by Charleston society, Ada ultimately is able to conclude that her education has sheltered her from the real world. Used to burying her head in a book, she initially shies from romantic involvement. By the novel's close, however, Ada has embraced both joy and pain. She has adapted to a life of manual labor, living according to the rhythms of nature. Ada has learned to find herself in the world by trusting in her intuition and heeding nature's unspoken signs. Ada's new existence thus requires her to have a deeper engagement with both the practical and emotional demands of life.

Ada's reunion with Inman testifies to her newfound openness. She overcomes her initial feeling of estrangement by addressing her fears and hopes for the future. Having laid roots in the community of Black Cove, Ada admits to Ruby that she fears a solitary future. However, the stark topography around Cold Mountain offers her sanctuary from feeling marginalized and eccentric. This landscape, moreover, provides a homeland she can share with Inman. After Inman's death, Ruby's family and Ada's own daughter continue to provide Ada with a source of emotional solace. In truth, Ada is not alone. Frazier demonstrates profound change in his female protagonist as she grows to find security living close to nature. In particular, the peaceful certainty of Ada's domestic routine indicates her comfort with the natural world's cycles and repetitions.

RUBY

Ruby is both a role model and a friend for Ada. As a strong-willed, practical woman with keen insight, Ruby initially serves as a foil for the dreamy, intellectual Ada. (A foil is a character that reveals the distinctive traits of another character through contrast.) Ruby's store of knowledge about the natural world teaches Ada to look outward from herself, and to interact with the surrounding environment. Ruby personifies many of the novel's themes about living close to nature, moving at pace with its seasons, and establishing a close relationship with the land. However, Ruby's role grows more substantial as Ada's character matures. As Ada develops into a strong friend and co-worker, the women's friendship becomes increasingly sisterly and profound. Just as Ada learns about practical life from Ruby, Ruby in turn learns from Ada, listening to the classic literature the older woman reads aloud and following her lead when it comes to expressing emotion (although emotional honesty does not come easily to Ada either). Resolutely levelheaded and self-sufficient, Ruby begins to let go of past resentment, particularly towards her father, and reclaims her faith in love.

Ruby's development within the novel, though not as dramatic as Inman's or Ada's, is far-reaching and profound. Ruby evolves from a girl into a natural mother figure. The novel charts her transition from someone who could function successfully outside of society as a hermit (she is similar in many ways to the goat-woman) to a woman who appreciates having her whole family living and working beside her. She is a matriarchal figure who keeps her husband and father in check without being too domineering. Ruby becomes the tie that binds her family together.

THEMES, MOTIFS & SYMBOLS

THEMES

Themes are the fundamental and often universal ideas explored in a literary work.

ISOLATION IN THE SEARCH FOR MEANING

The loneliness that many of the characters in the novel experience informs their search for meaning in a world torn by war and hardship. For example, Ada and Inman bury their feelings of isolation, just as they internalize their grief, regret, and hope for the future. Ada grows to feel content and secure at Black Cove but recalls the alienation she felt both on first arriving and immediately after her father's funeral. She also recollects her sense of estrangement from Charleston society. Similarly, Inman feels a sense of profound loneliness and growing misidentification with the human world because of his war experiences. His spiritual desolation is suggested when he listens to many people's tales of hardship but rarely shares details of his own past. Through his loneliness Inman cultivates an otherworldly spirituality, similar in many ways to the goat-woman's, that encourages people to talk. Frazier shows how Inman's solitude is not simply a physical state—it is a psychic introspection born from a need to find meaning in what appears to be a senseless existence.

However separated Inman feels from the human world, his character is not alienated from society. Even while he searches nature for some overarching spiritual truth, Inman recognizes that he seeks the solace of Ada's company. His journey becomes a solitary spiritual quest for communion with a greater power.

KNOWLEDGE AND INTUITION

The novel examines the area where intuition and knowledge overlap, particularly as this intersection touches on peoples' religious beliefs. The intellectual dictates of Christian society are seen as haughty and somewhat artificial in comparison to the oral traditions and cultural wisdom of more ancient civilizations and those with a connection to the land. Although he is not conventionally religious, Inman follows the Cherokee belief in a spiritual world. Inman uses these tales to intuit truths from nature—as demonstrated by his identification with the crow and the mountains of his homeland. Thus, Frazier shows Inman shaping his own conception of personal faith with reference to both received wisdom and intuition.

Ada re-evaluates both her intellectual and religious life in order to understand the relationship between objective knowledge and spirituality. Initially, she questions the merits of intellectualism in light of knowledge gleaned from sensory understanding. As the novel progresses, Ada embraces all that the land offers. She renounces the absolute authority of books in favor of intuition. Ultimately, she starts questioning her father's religious beliefs, concluding that the world around her is all that there is.

Generally, the characters balance an awareness and appreciation of received wisdom with intuition. They share a belief in their land and express this belief with reference to Christian doctrine, Cherokee tales, or their own personal creeds.

MOTIFS

Motifs are recurring structures, contrasts, or literary devices that can help to develop and inform the text's major themes.

SEASONAL CHANGES AND ROTATIONS

Frazier uses seasonal variation as an allegorical device to reflect the development of his characters. Ada, Inman, and Ruby seem to evolve in connection with nature's changes and cycles. Inman recognizes that his path is not strictly linear as he heads toward a place where past and present will meet. He even notes that his journey will be "the axle of my life." The revolving motion Inman experiences is underscored by the novel's treatment of time. Ada and Inman are haunted by memories—of themselves, each other, and their past—that bind them together and sustain their hope for the future.

The cycles of time are mirrored by nature's rhythms. The night sky represents a cosmic map that might foretell future events. Inman frequently observes Orion's path across the heavens and plots his own course by the location of sun and moon. As winter comes around, death settles on the landscape with an intensity that foreshadows Inman's own death.

THE PAST

The novel focuses heavily on the past—both before the outbreak of war and before Europeans colonized the Americans. For both Ada and Inman, the protagonists, what has already occurred resonates with undeniable authority. Ada thinks back on her childhood and reaches important conclusions about the forces, both helpful and harmful, that shaped her identity. Inman recalls both the horrors of war and the spiritual consolation provided him by Cherokee folktales. The arrowhead that Ada and Inman find symbolizes life's fleeting nature but also represents the potential for continuity and recurrence—Ada and Inman vow to return to see it in the future.

SYMBOLS

Symbols are objects, characters, figures, or colors used to represent abstract ideas or concepts.

THE CROW

Remaining true to its own cunning, the crow is a shifting and ambiguous symbol. Inman strongly identifies with this bird, looking to it with envy as a creature of independence, freed from the constraints that the world imposes. Ruby highlights the crow's merits when she points out its resilience and tremendous capacity for survival. While the crow suggests doom and destruction, it also demonstrates the dark instincts troubling man's soul.

FORKED ROADS AND CROSSINGS

Forked roads feature prominently in the text. Inman is often required to choose a direction or to take some course of action directed by the road ahead. Crossings symbolize the boundaries Inman traverses between the realms of the terrestrial and the spiritual.

DARK-HAIRED WOMEN

For Inman, dark-haired women symbolize Ada, the woman to whom he is returning. Each dark-haired woman is brave, self-sufficient and captivating. These women seem to act as beacons or markers along Inman's journey, leading him home to Ada.

Summary & Analysis

The Shadow of a Crow

He no longer thought of that world as heaven, nor did
he still think that we get to go there when we die.
Those teachings had been burned away.

(See QUOTATIONS, p. 57)

Summary

Inman wakes up in a hospital ward before dawn because his neck wound has attracted flies. The morning is too gray for him to see out of a window that usually provides him with a view of an oak tree, a road, and a brick wall. Inman gets up and sits in a chair. There he awaits sunrise. He imagines walking out of the window as he did when he first arrived at the hospital. Inman recalls a moment when he was bored with a history class at school. He threw his hat out the window. The hat was caught by the wind and landed at the edge of a hayfield, where it looked like a crow's shadow. The teacher threatened Inman with whipping, but Inman walked out of the classroom, retrieved his hat, and never returned.

Balis, the man in the bed next to Inman, wakes and begins working on translating ancient Greek texts. His right foot was blown off in battle, and his leg has rotted increasingly along its length. More people in the room begin to stir as the room lightens. Inman counts flies on the ceiling and waits for the blind man he has been watching for some weeks to arrive. He remembers the wound he received in battle near Petersburg. No one thought he would survive that wound. Before healing, the wound "spit out" small fragments of clothing along with something resembling a peach pit that caused Inman to have troubling dreams. Inman also recalls how he played a game while convalescing that involved counting time until a change occurred in the scene outside, framed by the open window.

The blind man arrives, and Inman goes to speak to him. Inman learns that the man has never had eyes and would regret gaining his sight for a brief time if it meant suffering its loss in the future. Inman replies that he wishes he himself had been blind at Fredericksburg when his regiment shot down thousands of Federal troops from behind a wall on a hill. He remembers "heaps" of corpses littering the battlefield as he went scavenging for boots; he also recalls a woman turned crazy by what she had seen and a soldier who killed a line of fallen Federals by smashing their heads in with a hammer.

Inman returns to the ward and opens his copy of Bartram's *Travels* at random. He loses himself in descriptions that remind him of his home's mountainous topography. A few days later, Inman goes into town to buy supplies, such as clothes and writing paper, with money sent from home and his back pay. He drinks bad coffee at an inn and reads in his newspaper about army deserters and Cherokee troops scalping Federals (Federal troops). Inman then remembers a Cherokee boy, Swimmer, whom he met when they were both sixteen and grazing heifers on the slope of Balsam Mountain. While they fished by a creek, Swimmer told Inman folktales and spoke of the nature of the soul. Next, Inman's coffee grounds and a flight of vultures make him think about divination. He remembers Swimmer saying that the mountains are gateways to a world above heaven where a "celestial race" lives. Responding to this comment, Inman pointed out to Swimmer that there was nothing at the top of Cold Mountain and other mountains he had climbed, although he could not discount the idea of a spiritual world invisible to the human eye.

Fiddle music draws Inman out of his reverie. He begins and then abandons a draft before mailing a letter that informs the recipient of his imminent return home. Inman returns to the hospital, finds that Balis has died, and reads Balis's translations. The day's sunset evokes in him a sense of grief. He adds his new supplies to his already-packed haversack and leaves that night through the open window.

ANALYSIS

Frazier opens the novel by introducing his brave yet haunted protagonist, a wounded Confederate soldier. He includes details of famous Confederate generals such as Lee and Longstreet to flesh out the historical framework of his narrative. However, the chapter focuses only indirectly on the Civil War and instead traces Inman's personal experience of it. Inman is clearly engaged with the world and seeks out other people in it. He is aware of Balis in the hospital bed beside him, just as he notes the changing view from his window and the movements of the blind man. Yet Inman is as troubled by the world as he is fascinated by it. His nightmares and lonely visions of the future suggest that he suffers from a psychological injury that will not easily heal.

Inman is in need of absolution from his past but does not know how to find relief. Inman cannot forget the atrocities that he has witnessed, particularly those that occurred in battle at Fredericksburg. Although he tells the blind man some of his war experiences, he does not share details of a recurring dream in which piles of human limbs reform themselves into "monstrous bodies of mismatched parts." Inman dreads the stare of a cadaver who speaks his name, leaving him to wake up "in a mood as dark as the blackest crow." In this chapter, the crow symbolizes Inman's independence, when he throws his hat out of the window as a boy, and it also symbolizes his internal disorder, when it is used as a simile for his dark mood. The crow reappears many times in the novel as an omen of doom, a symbol of independence, and a portent of change.

Inman is a man constantly on the move, a man who wishes to be reunited with his lover and who searches for the solace of human company. Despite his aversion to the "metal face of the age," Inman battles his own despair. He moves from his bed to the outside world, goes into town, returns to the hospital, and finally passes beyond its confines by stepping through the window. Frazier returns to this theme of crossing boundaries throughout the novel as Inman enters and exits different earthly and spiritual realms. Inman's flights of imagination and memories of a happier past are powerful tools that he uses to distance himself from the anguish he feels. Inman's love of Bartram's *Travels,* a book that he opens at random and gains comfort from, indicates his profound affinity for the natural world and for the movements of his book's "lone wanderer" author.

Frazier's contrasting descriptions of bloody battles and summer vistas underscore Inman's troubled and divided worldview. Despite his horrific experiences, Inman hopes for a better future. Inman abhors the idea that the soul is weak and mortal since he learned it by "sermon and hymn." This viewpoint juxtaposes Christian doctrine with a belief system formed from an individual's own experiences and desires. Inman assimilates or rejects other people's beliefs—be they the blindman's, Swimmer's, or Balis's—on the basis of whether or not they accord with his personal philosophy. The individual's evaluation of an idea's truth is important throughout the novel, as questions of religious and philosophical truth resonate with Inman as he searches for his own spiritual conclusions.

The first chapter is an aggregate of Inman's memories and experiences. It focuses on Inman's past, his search for answers, his yearning for a better life. Hope, or the tentative search for hope, is forcefully conveyed in this chapter and will emerge as one of the most powerful themes within the novel.

THE GROUND BENEATH HER HANDS

All of their Charleston friends had expressed the opinion that the mountain region was a heathenish part of creation. . . .

(See QUOTATIONS, p. 58)

SUMMARY

Ada sits on her porch writing a letter to Inman. She discards this letter and surveys her farm. She is hungry and concerned about managing the farm following her father's death. Ada looks for eggs and finds a hollow in a bush near a boxwood. Ada thinks back on her childhood in Charleston and regrets that the fine education she received is of no practical use. A rooster chases a hen into the hollow. The vicious rooster attacks Ada, and she leaves, nursing a cut wrist. She changes her clothes in the house and reads a book by an open window. Ada enjoys the view of Cold Mountain, but hunger soon forces her to look for food. After she fails at baking bread, Ada eats an unsatisfying meal of tomatoes and cucumbers. Then she walks to the church and puts flowers on the grave of her father, Monroe.

Ada thinks about her father's death in May. She remembers leaving him in the garden while she went to paint watercolors and finding him dead on her return. He was buried two days later. At the funeral, Ada decided to delay her return to Charleston. She stayed with her neighbors, the Swangers, for three days but was still afraid to return to the house in which she lived with her father.

Ada heads towards the post office. She meets three people, including a man who is ferociously "beating the shells off beans" as three crows watch impassively. She picks up a letter and goes to visit the Swangers, Esco and Sally. The two Swanger boys are off fighting in the war, but their parents do not support either side. Esco recounts a tale about a man named Teague and his band of Home Guard. Teague had tried to bully a family into handing over their valuables since the family was suspected of being in league with the Federals (the Union army). The husband had refused even as a guard tortured his wife. At the end of his tale, Esco talks about the "bad signs" he has heard of, including a talking owl and a sheep without a heart. The old man thinks these omens predict the war's encroaching path into the mountains. Also during this visit, Ada surprises Sally by saying that she is not yet ready to return to Charleston. Esco suggests that Ada look backward with a mirror into his well to divine her future. Ada sees a person walking but does not know whether this means she should stay and wait or follow the figure. The hymn "Wayfaring Stranger" comes into her head. Sally gives Ada some blackberry preserves when she leaves.

Ada walks back to the farm and climbs the ridge overlooking Black Cove. She remembers coming to Black Cove six years ago. She and Monroe (her father) had gotten lost and were forced to seek shelter in a church. The church turned out to be the new chapel where Monroe was supposed to begin preaching. Monroe was zealous in encouraging people to join, but many were "touchy and distant" and skeptical of the new arrivals. In fact, Monroe had caused offense by trying to convert the highly religious Swangers, thinking they were ignorant of the Gospel. He later apologized.

Ada pauses on a rocky outcrop on the ridge to read a letter from her father's solicitor informing her that his investments are worthless. Afterward, she heads down to the upper pasture and sits by a wall. Ada reads a book, falls asleep, and dreams that her father is a corpse in a train depot. He tries to tell her something, but she cannot hear him through the glass case. She awakens, watches the sunrise, and thinks about the future. She decides not to return to Charleston because the people there dislike her, and she would have to marry for convenience. Later that morning, a girl arrives at the farm, sent by Sally Swanger. She introduces herself as Ruby, and offers to help Ada on the condition that she is treated like an equal and "everybody empties their own night jar." Ruby decapitates a rooster and soon has broth simmering on the stove.

SUMMARY & ANALYSIS

ANALYSIS

The point of view in the second chapter shifts from Inman's to Ada's. Ada's perspective is notably calmer than Inman's. She ponders commanding mountainous scenery instead of the horrors of battle. However, like Inman, Ada must fight off despair. Although highly educated and literate, she is not used to manual labor and lacks the practical skills necessary to run a farm. In addition, the acute physical hunger Ada feels corresponds with her psychological yearning for the solace of human company.

Ada is filled with a desire to return home, or at least to discover where home might be. Like Inman, Ada is setting out on a journey, although she has little sense of identity or purpose. Ada surveys her land three times in this chapter, suggesting a budding relationship between her and the landscape. She recognizes that there is something rooting her to the farm. Her friendship with the Swangers, the memories of her father's happiness at Cold Mountain, and her own sense of security on the farm (which she feels when she hides within the boxwood and reads beside the wall in the upper pasture) make a strong impact on Ada. Frazier suggests that his female protagonist has a special connection to "her woods, her ridges, her creek."

Ada's vision in the well also encourages her to stay at the farm; it suggests she is awaiting someone's arrival. Although she dreams of Monroe calling to her, Ada seems more affected by the vision she sees in the well. This visualization foreshadows Inman's return. However, it also represents journeying or pilgrimage, an idea to which characters in the novel frequently return. This idea is reinforced by the hymn "Wayfaring Stranger" that haunts Ada's mind. Just as Inman sets out on his journey back home, so Ada tentatively takes her first steps towards living an independent life at the farm.

Ruby acts a foil for Ada. She is knowledgeable about nature and has an innate understanding of the way things work, while Ada is "filled with opinions on art and politics." Ruby, meanwhile, displays an outward authority that equals Ada's, though she is illiterate and plainspoken. Frazier shows throughout the novel how Ada and Ruby's relationship is based on terms of mutual respect and understanding, despite their obvious differences.

THE COLOR OF DESPAIR; VERBS, ALL OF THEM TIRING

SUMMARY: THE COLOR OF DESPAIR

Inman has been marching for days but is still near the hospital. He has dealt with the perils of bad weather, vicious dogs, and the threat of the Home Guard. Three men set upon Inman when he stops at a crossroads settlement to buy provisions. Inman steals a smith's scythe and beats all three before escaping into the woods. He chants the words of a spell Swimmer taught him. The words remind him of Monroe's sermon on Emerson and his discussion of why man was born to die. Inman heard that sermon the day he met Ada.

Inman remembers how he saw Ada in church and how he longed to touch the groove of her neck exposed by her hairstyle. A group of bachelors hung around after the service daring each other to talk to her. Finally, Inman persuaded Sally Swanger to introduce him. Their conversation was brief and awkward, although Inman surprised Ada by correctly constructing a simile.

Inman moves out of the pinewoods and follows the river. He thinks about becoming a hermit and living with Ada in the mountains to ward off despair. Inman reaches a ferry crossing and shouts across. A figure appears and uses a canoe to reach Inman. The rower is a young dark-haired girl who identifies the river as the "mighty" Cape Fear. Inman agrees to pay her twenty dollars for his ride, although the sign says five, because she is saving up to buy a horse and saddle on which to ride away. While they are paddling upstream, the three townsmen appear with several other men and start shooting at Inman. Inman and the girl jump into the river and use the sinking canoe for shelter and flow downstream, avoiding the men, who cannot see them in the dark. When they reach the riverbank, Inman pays for the damaged canoe, and the girl gives him directions to roads heading west.

Summary: verbs, all of them tiring

Ruby goes home to gather her belongings. She returns to Black Cove and makes an inventory of what needs to be done. Ruby decides that she and Ada will raise pigs, sell cider, and grow tobacco, among other things. She is pleased that Ada has no money since she distrusts it and is used to bartering goods. Ruby instructs Ada to choose either a piano or a cabriolet as an inessential item to be sold in order to support them through the winter. Ada chooses to barter the piano. Ruby barters it to a townsperson, Old Jones, for a sow, sheep, cabbages, and other goods. Watching it leave, Ada is reminded of a party Monroe threw the last Christmas before the war.

Inman arrived late the night of the party. Ada was shocked to find him drying the rain off his clothes in the kitchen. She had drunk too much champagne and found herself sitting in his lap. They did not talk much, but Ada remembers his damp wool smell and her feeling of contentment before she returned to play the piano in the parlor.

Ada rouses herself to search the basement for champagne. Instead of wine, she finds a sack of green coffee beans. The women stay up all night drinking coffee and talking. The next day Ruby barters the beans for chickens, vegetables, and salt. Ruby reiterates that she does not want to be treated like a servant and encourages Ada to share the work. The women settle into a domestic routine. In the evenings, Ada reads Greek tales out loud to instruct Ruby, beginning with Homer.

After dark, Ruby shares her life story with Ada. She relates that she never knew her mother and lived in a cabin with her "ne'er-do-well" father, Stobrod Thewes. Ruby was forced to be self-sufficient, as Stobrod left her for days at a time to "hunt" or party. One afternoon when Ruby was out foraging for food, she caught her dress on a briar and had to spend the night alone in the woods. Although she was only four, she heard a voice that made her feel watched over. Stobrod enlisted during the first days of the war, but his daughter has no idea what happened to him. Ruby believes that she is twenty-one years old but has no means of verification.

ANALYSIS: THE COLOR OF DESPAIR; VERBS, ALL OF THEM TIRING

As in the rest of the novel, in these two chapters, Frazier uses lyrical language to evoke the period and the setting. He does not write with the distant prose of a modern author. Inman describes the river as a "shit-brown clog" to his passage and exclaims "Shitfire" when he is attacked. Frazier's vocabulary—including terms such as "windage" and "grey tarboosh"—accords with Inman's perspective in the Southern states during the Civil War.

Inman crosses the first of many boundaries he will encounter, the Cape Fear. The river symbolizes movement and direction that reflects Inman's determination to return home. Inman crosses this river, leaving his violent acts behind. The reappearance of the three townsmen implies that Inman's past will catch up with him. The author suggests that Inman's progression cannot be strictly linear, as his journey across country draws out old memories and new hopes. Inman's mind turns to events of the past (the day he met Ada) just as he turns into the woods to avoid the townspeople and has to flow downstream to avoid getting shot. Even at this early stage, Inman recognizes that his journey will be "the axle of [his] life." This metaphor is ambiguous, for Inman could be alluding to the journey as a turning point, a pinnacle of achievement, or as a moment of revelation. In any case, Frazier develops his theme of pilgrimage in this chapter as a certain process leading towards uncertain ends. Inman is seeking convergence, but how he will find it, and with whom, has yet to be determined.

The next chapter shows Ada struggling to make sense of herself. She is surprised that living could be such a "tiresome business," but at least she is now required to do something that gives her life purpose. Ruby takes on a more defined role, as she makes plans and provisions for the winter. Ruby and Ada's efforts to ensure that they will survive the winter makes clear that food is a central concern of the novel. As a character, Ruby personifies many ideas about nature and the free soul that the author explores in Ada's experiences in "the ground beneath her hands." Ruby's experience in the woods as a young girl has tied her to the landscape in an indefinable way. Her insistence on sharing the farm work with Ada results from her awareness of the harmonies of nature, in which each element may be taken as part of a whole. The author returns to the broader theme of patterns, particularly their relation to meaning and to connecting past, present, and future at many points in the novel.

It is significant that Ada reads the *Odyssey* to Ruby. Homer's epic story of Odysseus's perilous pilgrimage shares many thematic and structural similarities with *Cold Mountain*. Events in Frazier's novel, such as Inman crossing Cape Fear, suggest that it parallels the *Odyssey*. Essentially, however, it is Inman's overwhelming sense of homesickness and loneliness, rather than similarities of plot structure, that links the two texts.

LIKE ANY OTHER THING, A GIFT; ASHES OF ROSES

SUMMARY: LIKE ANY OTHER THING, A GIFT

Inman follows the banks of Deep River at night. He sees a light ahead and worries that it is the Home Guard. Instead, he finds that it is a man who is about to throw a white bundle down the river gorge. The man thinks that Inman is a message from God. Inman pulls a gun on the man, who says that he is a preacher who has drugged his pregnant lover and was about to throw her into the gorge in order to kill her. Inman ties the man up and instructs him to lead them to his town. Inman cuts his thumb on the wire binding the horse's lead rope.

On the way back, the preacher reveals details of his affair. He states that he is engaged to someone else and that he would be exiled from his community if his infidelity were discovered. Inman sees that Orion has risen and remembers identifying a star in this constellation the night of the battle at Fredericksburg. The boy he shared this information with was dismissive of worldly knowledge, arguing that it lead to the carnage displayed on the battlefield. Although Inman had disagreed with the boy at the time, he now considers whether the boy might have been correct.

Inman can't decide what to with the preacher, and he tells him so. At the town, Inman gags his captive and ties him to a tree. Inman carries the woman to her bed in the cabin she shares with her grandmother. The girl wakes up, and Inman learns that her name is Laura. He tells her to go back to sleep and warns her against the preacher. Inman writes a letter detailing the preacher's criminal intentions and "skewers" it to the tree above his head. He leaves the town and sleeps in a pine bower.

When he awakens, Inman cleans his pistol and thinks how easily fighting comes to him. He leaves in the afternoon and continues walking. After an hour, Inman meets two slaves and follows the scent of meat to a camp filled by people as "Ishmaelite as himself." He eats stew, and watches a dark-haired woman ride a horse across the river. The woman reminds him of Ada. Inman shares frog legs with a band of gypsy boys and buys a bottle of Moet. He drinks some champagne and then goes in search of another meal from a man in charge of "show folk." Inman watches the man throw knives at the dark-haired woman. Later, the troupe eats beefsteaks and shares stories.

Inman is distracted by the beautiful woman and goes into the woods to rest. He reads a passage from Bartram's *Travels* about the rhododendron plant and drinks the last of the champagne. Inman's thoughts drift to Laura and how it felt to carry her when he did. He then thinks about the Christmas party and the conversation he had with Ada as she sat on his knee. Inman examined her hand for signs of the future but had found no "tidings" on it.

Inman falls asleep and dreams about Ada dressed in white with a black shawl. He tells her he is coming home and is never letting her go. Inman awakens to find the camp gone but sets off with lifted spirits, having had a pleasant dream.

SUMMARY: ASHES OF ROSES

Ruby and Ada hoe the garden and pull weeds. Ruby shares her belief in the "rule of the heavens" and how everything has grown in accordance with the "signs." Although Ada recognizes that Monroe would have dismissed these signs as superstitious, she sees them as metaphors.

A group of pilgrim women and children arrive from Tennessee. They say they are fleeing Federals who have burned their houses down. Ada and Ruby make them dinner. The next day, the pilgrims leave, and Ruby and Ada eat lunch in the orchard. Ruby tells Ada that she has learned everything she knows from observing nature and talking to old women and to Sally Swanger. Ruby shares some of her theories about nature, and Ada thinks about her own views of the world.

In the evening, Ada lets her mind drift and tells Ruby about the last party she attended in Charleston at her cousin Lucy's house. She wore a mauve dress that Monroe bought for her and went boating on the river with a man named Blount. Blount confessed that he was scared about the war, but Ada only could stroke his hand in response. On reentering the house, Ada became jealous of the confident woman she saw in the mirror, before she realized it was herself. Later, Ada found out that Blount had been shot in the face while walking backwards for fear of getting shot in the back.

Ada finishes her tale and thinks about Monroe's belief that the landscape around Cold Mountain is a reflection of another world. Ada decides that the physical world is all there is and goes to put her cow, Waldo, away.

ANALYSIS: LIKE ANY OTHER THING, A GIFT; ASHES OF ROSES

The chapter "like anything else, a gift" introduces the opposition between darkness and light. Inman stumbles across a man dressed in black who is about to kill an innocent woman dressed entirely in white. However, Frazier's narrative suggests that morality is not as clear-cut as this diametric symbolism might suggest. For Inman, there is a blurring between good and evil as he ponders what moral action he should take. By his own admission, Inman does not want to be "smirched" by other people's mistakes. Nonetheless, Inman is forced to witness the preacher's guilty confession and becomes embroiled in the man's moral dilemma. Throughout the novel, Frazier shows how Inman's instinct to do the right thing remains strong, even when he is required to kill to ensure his own survival.

Frazier introduces an element of light-hearted humor in this chapter. The preacher describes his assignations with Laura as "sport in a hayrick." When he states that he "anguished" over the situation on many nights, Inman responds that those must have been rainy nights when the hayricks were wet. Not only do such jokes enliven the text and emphasize the preacher's foolhardiness, they show that Inman has a sense of humor. Although it would appear to undermine the tragic focus of this chapter—an attempted murder—Frazier uses humor to highlight the light and dark aspects of human nature.

Inman meets a succession of female characters (beginning with the ferry girl in "the color of despair") that remind him of Ada. His reaction to each woman is one of suppressed longing, suggesting that he views her as an apparition of, rather than a replacement for, his distant lover. Frazier underscores Inman's fidelity to Ada; Inman does not attempt to satisfy his longing with the women he sees, although they elicit responses of buried desire. Inman's yearning for emotional and romantic solace is conveyed in his subsequent dream of Ada, in which he vows never to part from her.

The "ashes of roses" chapter incorporates the theme of Christian belief or received wisdom as opposed to intuition. Ada disagrees with her father's theology that nature's elements are mere "tokens" of another world. In addition, the pilgrims provide a background context for the war as they criticize the Federals for their cruelty. However, Frazier does not seem to be making an overt political point. The pilgrims symbolize the displacement brought about by war as their enforced journeying contrasts with Ada's newfound domestication. Ada herself is connected to the war only through the act of listening to other people's stories, past and present. She cannot assuage Blount's fear because she would consider such comfort artificial. Thus, while she is beginning to find contentment through industry, Ada, like Inman, bears witness to the cold realities of other people's lives.

EXILE AND BRUTE WANDERING

SUMMARY

Inman continues his journey. He asks a woman sitting on a porch in the fork of a road for directions to Salisbury. He steals lunch from a laundrywoman but leaves some money behind. Inman meets the preacher, who reveals his name to be Solomon Veasey, striding along the road. The preacher thanks Inman for saving him from sin, stating that he was thrown out of the community on account of his crimes. Veasey tells Inman of his plan to claim land in Texas and start up a cattle ranch. The two walk on together, although Inman does not want the preacher to accompany him. Veasey explains that he stole his revolver from an elderly neighbor.

The two pilgrims find an abandoned house where Inman forages for honey. They talk about sating their hunger, finding contentment, and God before they leave and follow the course of a stream. Veasey spies a catfish and insists on killing it. After Veasey dams the stream and unsuccessfully wrestles with the catfish, Inman shoots it in the head. The men camp for the evening and eat the fish. Veasey tries to draw out Inman's story, so Inman tells Veasey about a "blowup" at Petersburg. The Federals had successfully exploded a trench but were so shocked at what they had done that they found themselves routed by Inman's regiment.

It rains hard the next day. Inman and Veasey go into a store to buy supplies, but Veasey pulls his gun on the shopkeeper. Inman hits Veasey over the head and takes his pistol, and the men leave. A slave woman directs them to an inn where they can lodge for the night. A big "black whore" appears and identifies herself as Big Tildy. Veasey begins a quarrel with a customer over the whore. Inman and Big Tildy intervene to prevent him from getting shot. Veasey leaves to spend the night with Big Tildy, and Inman pays for dinner and a bed. He finds he is sharing the loft with a peddler called Odell. The man shares a flask of liquor with Inman and explains that he is heir to a plantation in Georgia.

Odell relates the unhappy story of how he fell in love with a slave, Lucinda, whom he wished to wed even though he was already married. Odell's father rented Lucinda to a farm when he confessed that he was in love with her. Nevertheless, Odell and Lucinda began an affair. When he discovered she was pregnant, Odell offered to buy the slave from his father, who asks cruelly whether he is buying her for the "fieldwork or the pussy." Odell punched him, and his father sent Lucinda to Mississippi. Odell was devastated and left home forever to look for the girl. He became a peddler in order to earn money to continue his search.

Odell and Inman drink more liquor. Odell describes some of the things he has seen on his travels, including a woman locked in a cage getting eaten alive by buzzards. After Odell determined that she wasn't Lucinda, the woman died on the ground in front of him.

The next morning Inman leaves the inn and meets Veasey. The preacher has a cut under his eye from Big Tildy but insists that the night has been worth it. He admits to being "stunned" by the sight of the naked prostitute.

ANALYSIS

As Inman's journey progresses, numbers and patterns arise with increasingly frequency within the text, and take on a mysterious significance. For example, an important pattern becomes evident as Inman finds himself noting the "pool of shadow" in a woman's lap above her splayed legs, revealed as she sits in the fork of a road. The junction of the road is echoed by the woman's posture, and both underscore the sense of partition and direction that guides Inman's journey. He knows that he cannot stay where he is, in a shady no-man's land, but must venture ahead one way or the other.

The crow motif reappears when a bird drops dead out of the sky in front of Inman, and a second time when three crows wait for catfish remains. Just as Inman's conscience weighs heavily with him, images of birds also overshadow the text. The crows echo the buzzards that feed off the caged and helpless slave girl in Odell's tale. The presence of the crows helps develop a theme of predation and threat as Inman becomes increasingly unsure of what to do in the face of cryptic and foreboding natural signs.

Inman's new insecurity is connected in part with the reckless preacher, who adds to the burdens Inman seems destined to bear. Veasey's reintroduction from the chapter "like any other thing, a gift" bridges Inman's past and present, suggesting that Inman distances himself from his past. Inman is obliged to intervene twice—at the store and at the inn—to save the preacher's life. Until Veasey's death, Frazier develops Veasey as a foil to Inman. For example, Veasey is someone who professes to have faith but really lusts after his own ends, while Inman consults his conscience before committing an immoral act. While the preacher is a self-serving individualist, Inman's conscience troubles him enough that he leaves money to pay for the laundry-woman's lunch. Also, Inman's alert but dispassionate response to violence is contrasted with the preacher's foolhardy, gun-toting bravado. In every respect, the travelers stand as a pair of opposites, echoing Ada and Ruby's contrasting relationship.

However, the author shows that Inman and Veasey share a similar hunger for spiritual salvation and contentment. This chapter strengthens the link between spiritual succor and physical nourishment. Both Inman and Veasey seek a more profound sustenance than that which food can provide. Hunger represents their need for absolution from past sins, and even the food they eat seems tainted. Their foraged honey is "toughened up" and black in color, and they find a blackbird and a hammer in the catfish's belly. Also, both characters desire to escape the hardship of their lives. While Inman becomes introspective and internalizes his fears, Veasey talks "on and on" by the river and sates his sexual desires with Big Tildy.

Frazier begins to explore the motif of narration, or the telling of tales, which weaves itself throughout this episodic novel. The author uses Odell's story to reinforce the fact that tragedies occur and lives go on independently of the Civil War, even if Inman personally has been shattered by his military experience. Frazier sets his characters against the backdrop of the Civil War, but ultimately *Cold Mountain* is a novel about people and landscape, rather than war or one historical event.

SOURCE AND ROOT

SUMMARY

Ada and Ruby walk into town. They observe and identify different birds. Ruby expresses her admiration for the crow, approving its cunning and ability to "relish what presents itself." Ada feels gloomy but explains her gloominess as a result of the manual work she's been doing, such as hay cutting, and the fact that it's raining. The women purchase supplies from the hardware store, and Ada buys *Adam Bede* from the stationers. They eat lunch by the river, before heading off to visit Mrs. McKennet, a local widow. Mrs. McKennet amuses Ada by recounting sensationalized war stories that she insists are true. Ada states that she finds war "degrading," and Mrs. McKennet affectionately calls her naïve. Ruby expresses her disinterest with regard to the conflict and dismisses Northerners as people who only worship money.

On the way home, Ada and Ruby pass the courthouse and stop to hear a captive narrate his tale. The prisoner describes how he was forcibly removed from his father's farm by a team of the Home Guard, led by the sadistic Teague. One of Teague's men killed the captive's father by impaling him with a sword; then Teague's other men ran three outliers out of the fodder crib. The captive was the only man to survive because he surrendered. Teague had considered hanging him anyway, but Birch, one of Teague's men, dissuaded him from doing so, saying it would look better if they brought someone in occasionally.

The man concludes his tale by stating that the world won't last long. Ada and Ruby return home, arguing whether one should take an optimistic or pessimistic view of the world. Ruby stops talking when she sees a heron. The women disagree over the bird's intentions before it flies off, and Ada sketches it from memory. Ruby tells Ada a story Stobrod told her, in which he suggested that her real father was actually a heron. In running to get away from the lusty bird, Ruby's mother crawled under the bed, got stuck, and was impregnated from behind. This story reminds Ada of Monroe's tale about how he wooed her mother, which she shares with Ruby.

Monroe had stopped to water his horse at a house outside of Charleston. He had fallen in love with the beautiful woman who had questioned him. He later found out that her name was Claire Dechutes and that her father was French. Monroe wooed Claire with her father's permission, on the condition that they marry after she turned eighteen. After a long wait, on the day he was due to propose, Monroe saw her kissing another man. Claire married the man and went to live in France while Monroe sought solace in England. However, Claire's marriage was unhappy, and she finally wed Monroe on her return from France nineteen years later. Two years later, Claire died giving birth to Ada. Despite his grief, Monroe had sworn to dedicate his life to his daughter.

When Ada finishes her tale, a flock of birds fly past the moon. Ada then correctly identifies the planet Venus, which is about to set behind Cold Mountain.

ANALYSIS

Ruby's "source and root" is that of the environment around Cold Mountain. Even if her father's tale about the heron is untrue, Ruby is a woman descended from the natural world who shares an affinity with its creatures. Whereas images of predatory birds such as the crow and buzzard overshadow Inman's journey, the women focus on birds attuned to their landscape as creatures of community and migration. Ruby's reassessment of the crow is important as it indicates the different perspectives that people can take on nature. While previous images of crows within the text have been shocking or disturbing, Ruby's frank assessment of the crow's gifts paints the bird in a different light, as a thing to be admired rather than feared. Throughout this chapter, Ruby is shown reading the signs of nature, as she speculates on a cardinal carrying a twig in its mouth and identifies the time of day by the angle of the sun.

If changes of nature form the steady background to this chapter, then tales of war dominate its foreground. The sadistic Teague reappears with his rabble of Home Guard who look like "battlefield dead." Yet, however ridiculous these men seem, their brutality exemplifies man's capacity for horror and perversity in times of conflict. The captive's tale foreshadows Inman's own experiences with the Home Guard in the next chapter and at the end of the novel. Also, as the novel suggests on other occasions, features of war point back to an earlier, primeval age. For example, the outliers carry old weapons that resemble "artifacts from a yet darker age." This descriptive detail continues the novel's theme of the past that will reach its apex when Ada and Inman find an old arrow head in the chapter called "the far side of trouble."

A striking feature of the captive's tale is how bleakly it contrasts with and refutes Mrs. McKennet's romanticized war stories. The "satisfied and plump" widow's glorification of war reminds Ada of Charleston society, as her tales lack any correspondence with actual events. Clearly, as Ada asserts, the conflict does not stand for principles of "tragedy and nobility." The military ideals the widow upholds are those Ada was unable to express to her friend Blount, as she remembers in the earlier chapter, "ashes of roses." Ruby's disinterest in the war underscores her dissociation from events and emphasizes the indifference of many Southerners toward the conflict. Frazier uses this chapter to explore the different reactions Southerners had to the Civil War, while focusing primarily on events in the natural world.

TO LIVE LIKE A GAMECOCK

He had grown so used to seeing death, walking among
the dead, sleeping among them . . . that it seemed no
longer dark and mysterious. (See QUOTATIONS, p. 58)

SUMMARY

Inman and Veasey come across a saw lying by a felled tree. Veasey steals the saw, justifying his actions by claiming that God shows little respect for property. The travelers eat the pods from a honey locust tree. They continue their journey, stopping to help a man who wants to remove a dead bull from a creek. Veasey unsuccessfully tries shifting the carcass according to his theory of fulcrums and leverage. Inman intervenes and uses the saw to dismember the bull. The men remove the body from the creek piece by piece. In gratitude for their help, the man offers Inman and Veasey dinner and lodging, which Inman accepts on condition that the man takes the saw. On their way to the man's home, the travelers stop and share tales over a bottle of liquor. The man identifies himself as Junior and tells a salacious story about his roving youth before complaining about his promiscuous wife and her two sisters.

The men arrive at Junior's tilted house, which has slipped its foundations. Inman and Veasey drink more and meet Junior's daughter, Lula. Inman stands on the porch and looks at the planet Venus before Junior introduces his wife Lila. Junior leaves to check on a horse, and Inman drinks earthy-tasting liquor with Lila and her sisters. He thinks that the children look "stunned." The women remove loaves baked in the shape of men from the fire. Lila explains to Inman that the disembodied light he sees in the forest is the ghost of a man Junior decapitated. Inman starts feeling dizzy and hides his haversack.

The women serve up an unidentifiable joint of meat for dinner "too big for hog, but too pale for cow," which Inman has difficulty carving. Lila tries to seduce Inman, but Junior walks in with his gun and says that he has brought the Home Guard. Inman and Veasey are arrested and bound to a line of other captives. Before the group leaves, Junior forces Veasey to officiate a marriage between Inman and Lila.

The men march eastward for days without food. Inman is depressed at the thought of retracing his steps. One night, the guards decide to line up the prisoners and shoot them, but Inman suffers only a superficial wound to the side of his head. Inman drifts in and out of consciousness before he is pulled from his shallow grave by hogs. Inman uses a stone to cut the rope binding him to Veasey's corpse. He commences walking westward and meets a slave, the yellow man, who gives him a melon. The slave offers the exhausted Inman a ride back to his owner's farm. Inman accepts. When the two reach the farm, the slave hides Inman in the fodder. There, Inman rests and loses track of time. When he decides to leave, the slave warns him to head north in order to avoid Confederate patrols, which are out looking for Federals. The slave draws Inman a map, explaining that his master has taught him to read and write. Inman thanks the man and regrets that he has no money to give him.

Inman returns to Junior's house, retrieves his haversack, and kills Junior by beating him in the head with his pistol. Inman walks westward all night and rests the next day under a tree in which three crows nest. Inman watches the birds and dreams of a world in which a man could transform himself into a crow and "fly from" or "laugh" at his enemies.

ANALYSIS

This central chapter of the book is concerned with repetition, rotation, and rebirth. Inman's identification of the planet Venus echoes Ada's identification of the same planet in the previous chapter. Frazier uses this detail to indicate how the couple's stories mirror and intertwine. More importantly, Inman changes his cardinal direction twice, sees Veasey die, and narrowly avoids death himself. Inman experiences a second resurrection when he is exhumed from his shallow grave. (His first resurrection was his extraordinary survival of the wound he took at Petersburg, related in "the shadow of a crow.") Inman is a changed man following his directional reversals and his near death. Not only does he commence his journey westward, he does so with a clear desire for vengeance. Inman's decision to kill Junior constitutes a moral climax in which Inman recognizes his need to kill in certain situations.

The novel's motif of darkness and light continues as Inman and Veasey are introduced to a world of darkness and depravity in which people are killed and eaten. In one of the novel's strongest parallels with the *Odyssey,* Lila appears in the same role as Homer's witch, Circe, a seductress who attempts to drug that epic's protagonist, Odysseus. Within this sinister environment, Inman seems pre-occupied with light. In his drug-induced, hypnotic state, he can focus only on the fire and light in the forest. After murdering Junior, Inman asks himself whether people's natures are all the same, with "little true variance." Although his motives for killing Junior are sound, Inman is clearly troubled by his act and feels numbed by it. Frazier suggests that Inman has returned to the same state of spiritual paralysis he felt after the battle of Petersburg. Inman's journey again turns back on itself, as he finds himself confronting deep psychological wounds that have not healed.

This chapter shows Inman searching for understanding in an increasingly chaotic world, as he struggles to leave the horrors of battle behind him. For Inman, the human world has begun to "scorn understanding"—even the patterns of the heavens no longer make sense. Frazier shows how close Inman's mind comes to breaking as his experiences run counter to reason. Seeking some sense of order, Inman turns to an augury for help—rather than to conventional religion—and tries to divine his future in the patterns made by melon juice. This continues the novel's theme of looking inward to one's own spirituality rather than outside to some higher power. Frazier reiterates that Inman is undergoing an internal spiritual journey as well as a physical geographical one.

The crow takes on a new symbolic significance for Inman as he identifies it as a spirit of autonomy, a creature that has the freedom to defy and mock its enemies. This new understanding of the crow is important because, throughout the novel, Inman is held at the mercy of his enemies, although he tries to reassert his will against fate. Significantly, the chapter ends with a complete blackout. This ending suggests that Inman's journey has become liminal: it has reached the threshold beyond which sensory perception fails. (*Liminal* means on the threshold of something, usually of some physical or physiological response.) The theme of liminality runs throughout the novel, reaching its apex in the chapter "spirits of crows, dancing," in which sensory perception fails Inman altogether for the final time.

IN PLACE OF THE TRUTH;
THE DOING OF IT

SUMMARY: IN PLACE OF THE TRUTH

Ada and Ruby lay fencerows with Ada's horse, Ralph. The horse is nervous, so Ruby blows into his nose to calm him down. Ada and Ruby find an old trap and set it to catch whomever has been stealing corn from the crib. Ruby leaves to trade goods with Esco, while Ada makes a scarecrow. She fashions its clothing out of the mauve dress she wore at her last Charleston party and uses a hat from France that Monroe gave her. Ada recognizes a group of crows and nicknames their leader "Notchwing." She eats lunch and sketches the scarecrow. Ruby returns with cabbages and hands a letter to Ada. The women bury the cabbages behind the smokehouse before they hold a contest to see who can braid the other's hair most intricately. Ada wins the contest and reads *A Midsummer Night's Dream* aloud before Ruby turns in for the night.

Ada reads the letter, which is from Inman. In it, he asks her not to look at his picture anymore because he has changed. Ada gets the photograph and decides it does not look like him anyway. She remembers nearly every soldier having his picture taken before he went off to war in 1861. Next, Ada thinks back on the last day she saw Inman, when they went walking by the creek. Inman told her an old Cherokee tale about an invisible world hidden in the mountains, a world free from pain that could only be entered on faith by those who had fasted for seven days.

Ada recollects the awkwardness of their goodbye and how she regretted not answering Inman's questions about what would happen if he died. Ada remembers she went to bed troubled and took the "easement" of "lomalakne love." She recalls how, the next day, she visited Inman in town and apologized for her behavior the previous day. The two kissed and parted at Inman's doorway.

SUMMARY: THE DOING OF IT

Inman follows the slave's map through hills to the mountain range drawn at its edges. He passes through "Happy Valley," which is actually miserable, and avoids patrols of the Home Guard. Inman follows a track through the forest and meets an old woman who offers him a meal. Inman follows her to her camp, realizing that he's climbed a river gorge, and looks at the mountains spread out in the distance. The lady's camp is a caravan surrounded by goats. The woman slaughters a goat and cooks the meat for Inman.

Over several days, Inman eats various meals made from goat meat and talks with the goat-woman. He pretends that he's been "furloughed" from the army on account of his wound, although the lady does not believe him. She tells the story of how she came alive alone in the woods after leaving her cruel husband.

Inman and the goat-woman discuss the war. The woman argues that the Southern army is fighting a godless war to protect slavery. She describes it as a "curse laid on the land." Inman talks further about his war experiences and states that men are drawn to fight by boredom rather than by an instinct of self-preservation. The woman gives Inman herbal remedies to heal his wounds. He and the goat-woman drink bowls of laudanum, and Inman surprises himself by talking about Ada. Inman considers living a hermetic existence like the goat-woman's but concludes that it would be too lonely. The old woman explains that she keeps a record of her life by writing and painting but does not say who taught her to read and write. The characters talk about dying alone, and the woman explains that she does not want to after she cannot fend for herself.

The next day, the goat-woman tells Inman a tale about a deal she struck with a man in town who refused to let her keep the bells on the goats that she was giving him. Inman falls asleep and awakens at night surrounded by goats. He searches in the woman's journals and finds many drawings of goats. The goat-woman returns, warns Inman to be careful, and gives him a drawing of a carrion flower before he sets off.

ANALYSIS: IN PLACE OF THE TRUTH;
THE DOING OF IT

The chapter "in place of the truth" highlights Ada's increasing awareness of her environment, as she starts nicknaming crows she sees around the farm. The female protagonist's decision to dress a scarecrow in her mauve dress and fancy hat shows her distance from the concerns of society. Frazier indicates how close Ada and Ruby have become as they braid their hair and compliment each other. The author juxtaposes Ada's memories about the last days she spent with Inman against this background of friendly intimacy. Her memories of Inman indicate the deep current of longing that passed between the lovers and which continues to hold them together.

Both "in place of the truth" and "the doing of it" develop the novel's commentary on spirituality by exploring the possible existence of an invisible world lying parallel to the visible one. The Cherokee woman's tale that Inman recalls echoes Swimmer's ideas about mountains as gateways to a celestial world (ideas that Inman recollects in the chapter "the shadow of a crow"). This tale is, as Ada rightly interprets, about Inman's "fears and desires," particularly as he fears losing something he values (Ada) through his own misdeeds. Just as the people in the tale desire an existence free from the ills and strife of their world, so the story hints at Inman's need to find spiritual peace and sanctuary.

This search for a better existence is developed in "the doing of it," in which the goat-woman appears as a kindred spirit to Inman. Because of his harrowing experiences in "to live like a gamecock," Inman shows resolve to distance himself from the evils of mankind. Although Inman wonders whether he is capable of living alone like the old woman, he clearly respects her resilience and survival instincts. The anonymous goat-woman is spiritual in the sense that she knows the secrets of nature. She heals Inman with herbs and feeds him with meat raised by the land. The woman, like the "yellow slave" who gave Inman his map in the preceding chapter, possesses wisdom and intuition. She is literate and has opinions about events in the world (such as the war), but she is driven to live outside of human company. Frazier suggests that the goat-woman acts as a bridge between the natural world and the world of man.

In many ways, Inman also is bridging both worlds. He is searching for a convergence between the horrors of his past and the hope of a better future. Perhaps this search leads him to confide in the goat-woman about his love for Ada and his vision of their eventual marriage. Inman uses the analogy of paired lines to describe his hope for this union, which will draw them together to form "one line" instead of two. This is the first time that Inman discloses his feelings about Ada and his hopes for the future to another person. It is significant that he should share this information with a woman who herself longs for an absent lover, a "yellow-haired" boy whom she abandoned to marry her cruel husband. Ironically, the goat-woman has decided upon a life of isolation in order to forget about her loneliness. In contrast, Inman believes that only living with Ada will console his spirit.

FREEWILL SAVAGES;
BRIDE BED FULL OF BLOOD

SUMMARY: FREEWILL SAVAGES

Ruby finds a man caught in the corncrib trap. She recognizes her father, Stobrod Thewes, and deduces that he has been stealing grain to brew liquor. Ruby makes him breakfast, but she draws the line at inviting him into the house. Stobrod tells Ada and Ruby that he is living in a mountain cave with a group of outliers. He leaves, and the women walk to the barn to check on the tobacco leaves. Ruby insists that the tobacco leaves are thriving because they have been grown and harvested in accordance with "the signs." Ada and Ruby then sit in the hayloft, and Ada fails Ruby's test to see whether she can identify different trees by the sounds of their leaves.

The women have supper outside, and Strobod reappears. He shows the women an unusual fiddle he made himself. Instead of a scroll, it has the head of a snake. Stobrod explains how he hunted a rattlesnake and put its rattle into the body of the fiddle, so that his music would have the "dire keen of snake warning." Ruby remains skeptical, and Stobrod tries to convince her by playing some tunes. He says that he began to compose his own music after a dying fifteen year-old girl asked him to play her a tune of his own. The tune Stobrod came up with is now so ingrained in Stobrod's mind that it has become a force of habit. Stobrod finishes by talking about the satisfaction he receives from the formation of harmonies. He plays a song called "Green-Eyed Girl," which is mainly about yearning. Ruby says it is surprising that Stobrod has found the only "tool" he is good at this late in life, and she explains how he got his nickname after being beaten with a "stob" for stealing. Ada thinks that Stobrod's change of character is miraculous.

SUMMARY: BRIDE BED FULL OF BLOOD

Inman wanders in the woods without any guidance from the sun or the night skies. His wounds heal, but he becomes ravenous with hunger. Inman wishes he could grow wings and escape from human society altogether, although he imagines men would come to his hermitage to convince him otherwise. While he is walking by a creek, Inman meets a strange little man who identifies himself as sympathetic to the Federals. Inman states that he has no affinity for either side, and the man admits that he has none either since his son was killed in battle. The man's name is Potts, and he directs Inman to a nearby house where he can get a meal.

Inman arrives at the house and meets a young brown-haired woman who cooks him a meal. This woman, Sara, is eighteen and explains how her husband died fighting in Virginia before he got to see their baby. Inman is depressed as he realizes the depth of her despair. Sara gives Inman her husband's clothes in return for his offer to slaughter her hog. That night, she asks Inman to sleep in her bed and tells him her sad story. Inman's sleep is fretful and troubled by dreams that the creatures on the quilt are chasing him.

The next day, three Federal soldiers appear, and Sara tells Inman to leave. He hides in the woods and watches as the soldiers threaten the young woman and demand money. When she explains that she doesn't have any, the soldiers take her hog and some chickens. Inman watches them leave, tells Sara to boil water and follows the men as they continue on their journey. He listens to the soldiers talk about their homes in New York and Philadelphia. He shoots all three after discovering that the man who threatened Sara is called Eben. Inman thinks about what he has done and concludes that he has committed worse acts. He returns to Sara's home with the hog and three chickens.

Inman and Sara eat the chickens for lunch and slaughter the hog. Sara makes supper, and Inman shaves. That night, Inman watches as Sara nurses her sick baby and sings a lullaby that includes the words "bride bed full of blood." He thinks about the young woman's bravery, and the two fall asleep together. Inman leaves the next day.

SUMMARY & ANALYSIS

ANALYSIS: FREEWILL SAVAGES;
BRIDE BED FULL OF BLOOD

Stobrod's return and his connection with a community of outliers both disrupts the calm continuity of the women's lives and shows the novel's thematic opposition between the natural and man-made worlds. His sudden appearance at the fodder crib reminds Ada and Ruby that not all events may be explained by reference to the natural world—they had assumed that a small creature had been stealing their corn—but instead that men can manipulate, change, and sometimes threaten. Although Ruby is wary of helping her father, Ada's generosity in sharing food with Stobrod shows her new openness of character and interest in her friend's family.

One way that the novel follows through on its exploration of the differences between man-made and natural phenomena is by focusing on music, which plays an important role in these chapters. Stobrod's repertoire of 900 fiddle tunes foregrounds the motif of sound and harmony that runs through the text. Ruby's father talks about the tune he played to the dying girl, a melody that has now become a "habit" and that serves to give "order and meaning to a day's end." Ada finds it remarkable that music has redeemed Stobrod, even if this is only a partial redemption, and remains optimistic that everyone can make something of his or her life. Frazier shows how Stobrod has found something to give his life meaning, a thing for which both Ada and Inman are searching. Music also appears as a backdrop to Ada and Ruby's natural environment. The dry scratching of the leaves in the trees is much like the snake rattle in Stobrod's fiddle, although it does not carry the same sense of alarm or warning.

Music is similarly important in the "bride bed full of blood" chapter. Sara's singing holds Inman's attention because the words of her lullabies are full of pain and horror. Frazier suggests that, because tragedy is all Sara has known, it is all that she can sing about. Inman interprets her singing as a sign of her bravery. He identifies in it a touch of the "specter world," a comment that calls to mind his belief in an invisible world. The routine that Inman and Sara develop—of lying beside each other in Sara's bed like husband and wife—is both powerful and pathetic. It symbolizes a comfortable and content domesticity that Sara never again will know. Once again, Inman's journey draws him into a world of pain in which he bears witness to the sadness and hopelessness of other people's lives.

However, Inman is prepared to act as well as to listen. Inman realizes that he has to kill the three Federal soldiers so that Sara and her baby won't starve. Although this act troubles Inman, he recognizes that he has suffered and seen worse acts committed in the name of war. Just as Inman killed the immoral Junior in "to live like a gamecock," here he brings retribution to the Federal soldiers. Frazier casts his protagonist in the light of an avenger concerned with equalizing some of life's inequalities. Inman's acts prove that he has not lost the warrior instinct that preserved him in battle and that now fires his determination to return home.

A SATISFIED MIND; A VOW TO BEAR

SUMMARY: A SATISFIED MIND

Keeping track of [the sun] would be a way of saying,
You are here, in this one station, now. It would be an
answer to the question, Where am I?

(See QUOTATIONS, p. 60)

Ada is contented with the relatively easy work of harvesting apples. Ruby leaves to trade cider for beef, leaving her friend to split logs and make a bonfire with dead brush. Ada tires herself chopping the logs, and she decides to write to her cousin Lucy. She explains how much she has changed physically and emotionally—she can now appreciate nature without one idea passing through her head. Ada realizes that she has not mentioned Ruby at all in her letter and puts it aside. She returns to her fire, milks the cow Waldo, and reads *Adam Bede*. Ada thinks about clearing a space in the trees along the ridge to mark the sun's highest and lowest setting points during the year.

Stobrod and a young man walk up to Ada. The three sit around the fire drinking, and Stobrod introduces his friend Pangle, a fellow outlier. Ruby's father describes how he stole a banjo, which he gave to Pangle, during a raid on a man's house. Since the young man displayed a natural talent for playing the instrument, the two became a duo. Ruby returns and puts the beef joint she has with her into the fire to cook. Stobrod and Pangle play and sing in unison. Ada is moved by the strange music and by Stobrod's obvious pleasure in performing it. Afterward, everyone eats dinner, and Stobrod asks his daughter to give him provisions and let him hide out occasionally at the farm. He says he fears that Teague will hunt down the outliers because of their raiding. Ruby says that it's not her place to agree to his request and looks to Ada to answer. She is dismayed when Ada agrees. Ruby explains how Stobrod abandoned her for three months when she was a child to start a business distilling liquor on Cold Mountain. Ruby concedes that he never hurt her but qualifies this by saying he never touched her in kindness either.

The men leave, and Ada looks up at the night sky. She retrieves Monroe's spyglass and observes a lunar eclipse. Ada wishes she could express what is in her heart honestly and directly. This inspires her to write Inman a one-line letter, which reads, "Come back to me is my request."

SUMMARY: A VOW TO BEAR

Inman meets a woman whose daughter has just died. He helps the lady bury her child and eats a meal she prepares. He looks at a picture—described as an "artifact"—of the woman's large family, of which she is now sole survivor. Inman continues walking and spends a night in an old chicken house. When he awakes, he reads a passage from Bartram's *Travels* describing the topography surrounding Cold Mountain. The next day, Inman finds three skeletons hanging from a tree and listens to the musical "tock and click" of their bones.

Later, Inman walks along a ridge in the mountains near home. He sets up camp atop a "rocky scarp" and is awakened in the night by an angry bear and her cub. Inman is reluctant to shoot the creature, recalling a vow he had made when he was younger. Inman puts aside his pistol and tries talking to the bear, but she lunges nevertheless. Inman deftly steps aside, and the bear plunges down to the rocks below. Because he feels that there is nothing else he can do, Inman shoots the bear-cub in the head and eats it. Guilt-stricken by his act, Inman describes the meat as tasting "like sin." Since he cannot decide which of the seven deadly sins he has committed, he creates an eighth, "Regret," to describe how he feels about his act.

ANALYSIS: A SATISFIED MIND; A VOW TO BEAR

Death features prominently in both of these chapters. As the seasons turn towards winter and the days are "snuffed out" earlier, Ada thinks about the changes that have occurred within herself and in the natural world. She burns dried grasses and acknowledges that she has changed beyond recognition. As Ada watches the sunset and the lunar eclipse, the author suggests that even the movements of celestial bodies seem prophetic of death or change. Ada's contemplation of the "looping" of the years, and her decision to clear the trees along the ridge to mark the sun's highest and lowest setting points suggest that Ada is beginning to think about a long-term future at Black Cove. Her thoughts have turned toward continuation and repetition, in keeping with the cycles of nature. She finds a peaceful certainty in the thought of tracking the progress of the years by these cycles, so that they cease to be an "awful linear progress" and instead become something whole, complete, and consistent. Indeed, Ada's focus on natural cycles will intensify, and it will help her to deal with her life's uncertainties. In the novel's final chapter, "epilogue. October of 1874," Ada will hold on to nature's habitual and pre-determined variations in consolation for the changes of a capricious and unpredictable world.

Ada's appreciation of natural rhythms extends to an enjoyment of Stobrod and Pangle's strange yet harmonious music. When they play, the two musicians achieve a kind of unity that has an almost mystical power over Ada. However, the "deep place of concord" that they find while performing only highlights the discord that they have encountered in the mountains. Stobrod's stories about the outliers' raids show how conflict has encroached on the peaceful solitude of mountain life. Once again, the war forms a stark backdrop to human relationships in the novel—Stobrod contacts Ruby because he needs her help, not because of any patriarchal concern. Nevertheless, their reunion marks the beginning of reconciliation between the two that Frazier develops in later chapters. Frazier shows how Ada is eager to aid the growth of Ruby's relationship with her father—she states that it is a daughter's "duty" to help her father—in part because she no longer has a father of her own to whom she can turn.

As he journeys home, Inman continues to face the reality of death at every turn. Inman sleeps among chicken droppings that smell like the "dusty remainders of ancient deadmen." He encounters skeletons, kills two bears, and buries a young girl who leaves her mother all alone in the world. As Frazier shows throughout the novel, death pervades Inman's world. However, it still retains its power to shock him; Inman experiences a moral quandary when he kills the bearcub. Something spiritual in Inman dies alongside the bear. Inman's overwhelming feeling of "regret" points to a deeper sense of culpability about his past actions. It appears that Inman cannot forget what he has done even as he nears Cold Mountain. Rather ominously, death and killing seem to be following him home.

NAUGHT AND GRIEF; BLACK BARK IN WINTER

SUMMARY: NAUGHT AND GRIEF

Stobrod, Pangle, and a third man climb the lobe of a mountain. They all have digestive problems from venison they have eaten the day before and often have to rush off into the bushes. The men find level ground and pause, determining which way they should go. The third man is identified as a fellow outlier, a boy of seventeen from Georgia whose cousin recently died atop Cold Mountain. Stobrod and Pangle are looking to start their own community near the Shining Rocks. They gather provisions that Ruby and Ada left for them underneath a stone covered with strange markings.

The men discuss which trail to take. Stobrod decides that they should eat a meal before deciding how to proceed. The boy disappears into a thicket on account of his "scours" from the venison while Stobrod dozes in front of the fire. He awakens to find a troop of Home Guard with their weapons drawn on him. Teague tells the men he knows they're deserters and that he's looking for the outliers' cave. Stobrod lies to Teague and gives a false location, but Pangle reveals where the cave is when Teague questions him. Teague and his men cook breakfast. Stobrod tells Teague what he's been up to and then plays some tunes with Pangle for entertainment. Birch calls the musicians "holy men" before Teague tells them to stand in front of a nearby poplar. Stobrod holds his fiddle proudly in front of him while Pangle gives his executioners a friendly smile. Unnerved, Teague orders Pangle to hold his hat in front of his face before the guards shoot both him and Stobrod.

SUMMARY: BLACK BARK IN WINTER

The Georgia boy recounts the tale of Stobrod's and Pangle's deaths to Ada and Ruby. Ada asks the boy why he wasn't killed, and he explains that he was hiding in the thicket. Ada asks him to show them the way after promising to feed him. Ruby displays no sign of emotion; she decides that the men should be buried up the mountain. Ruby explains to the boy the route he needs to take to get home. The women plan their journey and decide they will have to spend a night in the woods. They dress in Monroe's old clothes and leave the farm.

Ada and Ruby walk through the gloomy woods. Ada disagrees with her father's theological reasoning that everything in the world holds its own heavenly meaning. It starts snowing and the women search for shelter. Ruby finds a camp that she remembers from her childhood. The women eat and rest underneath a stone shelter. They find traces of ancient civilizations, including fragments of arrowheads in the ashes of the fire. Ada watches the patterns of light thrown by the fire. Ruby argues that mankind never advances, but loses something for everything that it gains.

The next day the women reach the trail fork and find Pangle. They decide to bury him near a chestnut tree, and Ada hopes that the locust cross they use will grow and tell a tale like Persephone's, with "black bark in winter" and white flowers in the spring. Ada finds Stobrod, who is still breathing. Ruby removes the bullet from his chest. The women descend into the valley and set up camp in an old Cherokee village. They put Stobrod to bed in one cabin and stable Ralph in another. Ada stares at the fire and feels overcome by loneliness.

ANALYSIS: NAUGHT AND GRIEF;
BLACK BARK IN WINTER

In the chapter "naught and grief," music appears to provide a measure of harmony if not logic in a world of insensible changes. Teague and the Home Guard are moved by Stobrod and Pangle's performance, although they shoot the musicians nonetheless. This brutal act is committed out of fear and a lack of understanding, and it foreshadows Inman's eventual death.

Trails and pathways feature heavily in "naught and grief" and in "black bark in winter," continuing a motif of orienteering that runs throughout the novel. For example, in the previous chapter, "a vow to bear," Inman returns home by following an old trail into the mountains. Similarly, in "naught and grief," Stobrod and Pangle search for the path to Shining Rocks. Later, Ada and Ruby plan their own trail into the mountains, and Ruby tells the young man the way to Georgia. In following historic routes that others have trod before him, each character belongs to both the present and the past—each effectively becomes a timeless traveler. Both the men and the women find Cold Mountain covered with traces of an older civilization. Arrowheads, "Indian" trails and stone slabs covered with ancient writing symbolize a lost world that time has placed out of reach. Frazier uses these archeological objects to reintroduce the idea of man as a being who leaves only traces of his presence in the world. This chapter questions whether man evolves or regresses over time, or whether things simply change. Ruby's philosophy is clear—she thinks that mankind loses and gains as time passes and that men and women will be lucky to "break even" in the future.

Ada's contemplation of the congruence of heaven and earth, and of the deeper meaning behind seasonal changes, contrasts with Ruby's philosophy. Ada remembers her father's tendency to allegorize every feature of nature after consulting a book written for this purpose. According to his book, everything has its own deeper meaning. For example, a crow would represent the "dark forces"

waiting to take over a man's soul. Ada rejects such allegorical inter-
pretations of the world, as she now regards information from books
to "lack something essential." In this way, Frazier shows how Ada
has grown to trust her own senses and to intuit rather than reason
out truths about the world.

Frazier suggests that Ada equates change with uncertainty.
Clearly troubled, Ada stares into fires and has visions in her dreams.
For example, she considers whether past inhabitants of the abandoned Cherokee village ever predicted that they would be forced
into exile. She remembers lyrics from one of Stobrod's songs about
a mole and the agony of lost love. The wonder and horror of the
song unsettle her. Ada seems deeply perturbed by the sliding scale of
life's experiences—its pleasures, pains, and unaccountable changes.
Although the female protagonist is happy on the farm, her anxiety
for Inman clouds her contentment. Even the landscape suggests this
duality as pristine snow falls around black trees. Like life itself, the
world is filled with stark contrasts.

FOOTSTEPS IN THE SNOW;
THE FAR SIDE OF TROUBLE

SUMMARY: FOOTSTEPS IN THE SNOW

Inman finds the camp where Pangle died. He sees the women's
tracks but postpones following them because night is drawing in.
Inman feels empty with hunger but vows not to eat anything until
he finds Ada. Inman remembers his arrival at Black Cove that
morning and how it had differed from the way he had imagined it.
The Georgia boy informed him of events and explained that the
women had set off up the mountain. Inman rests in front of the fire
and hopes that Ada will "redeem" him when he finds her. He
thinks about preachers such as Veasey and their false promises of
salvation. Nevertheless, Inman holds out faith that he can be
saved. He sets out at dawn to follow the tracks in the snow. When
a fresh snowfall arrives and fills in the footprints, Inman shelters in
a hemlock grove in despair.

Ruby wakes up to find that Stobrod is feverish and decides to
make him a poultice (a cloth used to soothe a wounded or aching
part of the body). Ada leaves to hunt turkeys and manages to kill a
pair with one shot. Inman leaves the grove when he hears the gunshot. He sees a man standing with a gun before realizing that he sees

Ada. Ada does not recognize Inman and states that she does not know him. Inman turns to leave but thinks better of it; as soon as he speaks, Ada recognizes him. She picks up the turkeys, and the two return to camp. Inman listens as Ada talks reassuringly about anything that comes into her head.

SUMMARY: THE FAR SIDE OF TROUBLE

> *All you can choose to do is go on or not. But if you go*
> *on, it's knowing you carry your scars with you.*
>
> (See QUOTATIONS, p. 61)

Ada, Inman, Ruby, and Stobrod sit together in a cabin. The men go to bed, and the women clean out and repair another hut. Ada finds an old wooden bowl and sets it in a niche. They roast the turkeys, and Ruby tells Ada that she doesn't need Inman. Ada replies that she doesn't want to become an "old bitter woman."

Inman wakes up and brings Stobrod water from the creek. He enters the women's hut and eats some cooked turkey. Ruby makes broth for her father and leaves, saying that she might be gone for a while. Inman does not know what to say, so he reads Ada a passage from his copy of Bartram's *Travels*. Embarrassingly, the passage he chooses is about sex. Inman leaves to scour his dishes in the river, but the memory of Ada's touch draws him back to the cabin. He and Ada hold each other while Ada summarizes the letters she wrote him. Inman fears he may be "ruined beyond repair." The lovers talk about the future and the people who might have lived in the cabin. Ruby returns, and Inman leaves. Ada tells Ruby that Stobrod can recover at Black Cove farm.

The next day, Ada and Inman go hunting for game but find nothing. Ada explains that she wants to keep Ruby around the farm. The couple comes across an old arrowhead buried in a poplar tree while searching for medicinal herbs. They discuss returning to this place in the future with their family to observe the arrow shaft's decay. Ada and Inman return to camp and the men go to bed. Ada and Ruby discuss their vision "of plenty" regarding the farm. That night, Ruby stays beside her father, and Ada and Inman sleep together. Later that night, the lovers talk about their childhoods and the past. Inman does not talk much about the war because he recognizes that no description, however detailed, could convey the truth of it. Instead he tells Ada about the goat-woman and his long journey home. Inman and Ada discuss their marriage plans and how they will live at Black Cove in the future. Inman resolves to learn Greek and play music.

ANALYSIS: FOOTSTEPS IN THE SNOW; THE FAR SIDE OF TROUBLE

In many ways, Inman and Ada's reunion is anti-climactic. Put simply, Ada is not where Inman expected her to be. Instead of striding heroically into Black Cove, Inman is forced to climb Cold Mountain looking haggard and dejected. Ada herself is wearing pants, not the delicate "ankle boots" and "petticoats" Inman had anticipated. The changes in the physical appearances of both characters signify the internal changes they have undergone. Inman recognizes that a life with Ada is his journey's true destination, rather than his family (of whom he makes no mention) or even the landscape. Inman admits his fear that Ada will "recede before him forever" leaving him a "lone pilgrim." This anxiety has defined their relationship from the start, as both have sought to overcome their shared emotional reserve and inclination toward privacy. The effects of Ada and Inman's estrangement are conveyed in the initial awkwardness of their greeting. However, the sincerity of their feelings toward one another soon resurfaces as each gains the courage to reach out to the other.

Footsteps and tracks feature prominently in this chapter as symbols of impermanent guidance. The prints are temporary marks, traces that vanish while nature's cycle continues. Inman's emptiness and hunger suggests his need for spiritual as well as physical sustenance. The novel's treatment of hunger as a metaphor for all kinds of need culminates in this chapter, in which Inman eats real food and reunites with Ada. For once, he feels sated. Hope is born again, although it cannot undo all the anguish he has suffered.

The theme of change dominates in "the far side of trouble." Both characters recognize that they have changed, but Ada asserts that perhaps she likes "them both better." The lovers discuss the future and their past experiences. Ada and Inman's new shared optimism is shown by their response to the antiquated arrowhead. Inman's reaction is not what it once would have been. Whereas he previously viewed old artifacts as symbols of primitivism, he now sees the arrowhead as a symbol of continuity, something that he and Ada can show to their children in the years ahead.

SPIRITS OF CROWS, DANCING;
EPILOGUE. OCTOBER OF 1874

SUMMARY: SPIRITS OF CROWS, DANCING

Ada and Inman wake up to their third day in the village. They decide that the war cannot go on for much longer and that it will be over by late summer. Inman rejects the option of returning to the army, and Ada vetoes the idea that he should hide as an outlier at Black Cove because of the danger involved. They settle on their third option, that Inman should walk north and surrender to the Federal army. The two promise to stay faithful to their vision of the future. Meanwhile, by the fourth day, Stobrod can sit up by himself. His wounds look almost healed, and he starts eating solid food. Ada watches as the other three devour cooked squirrels. She does not eat because she is put off by the fact that the squirrels still have teeth.

The snow starts melting on the morning of the fourth day when Ada and Ruby leave for Black Cove. Inman decides to follow later with Stobrod; the men do not want to jeopardize the women's safety on their journey. Inman resolves that he will hide out one night in the woods before heading north. The women leave, and Inman watches some of the "richness of the world" disappear along with Ada. He loads Stobrod onto Ada's horse, and the men follow. When they pass Pangle's grave, Stobrod remembers of his friend.

Continuing along the trail, the men hear noises behind them. They turn to see Teague, a boy, and some other men. Inman realizes there is no point reasoning with these men. He hits Ada's horse to send Stobrod "bucking off" into the woods and out of danger. Inman then shoots a wolfhound and one guard. The other men rein in their scared horses. Recognizing that there is nowhere that he can take cover, Inman shoots another man off his horse. One guard is crushed by his horse; meanwhile, the boy rides off into the woods. Teague threatens Inman with his knife before Inman shoots him in the chest. Inman hits the downed man with the butt of Teague's rifle. He finds the final rider—the boy—nearby in the woods, hiding on his horse behind a tree. The boy, Birch, admits that he will come looking for Inman if they both live. Birch's horse bolts, and he falls to the ground. As Inman tells Birch to put his pistol down, Birch shoots Inman.

Ada hears the shots and sees Stobrod. She rushes back to find Inman sprawled on the ground and holds him in her lap. Inman sees a vision of crows and all the seasons blended into one. The narrator describes this scene as if watching from a ridge, explaining how content the lovers look from afar.

SUMMARY: EPILOGUE. OCTOBER OF 1874

Ada thinks about Ruby's happy marriage to the Georgia boy, Reid. She watches her friends' children play in the yard. Ada thinks on the seasons—how she tries to like winter but in fact loves autumn best. Ruby comes out of the kitchen with a nine-year-old girl. The large family sits down to eat with Stobrod, who has just finished milking the cow.

Later that evening, everyone gathers around the fire. Stobrod plays his fiddle while the children play and run around. The girl is scolded for waving a burning stick and responds by kissing Ada and calling her "Mama." Ada reads the children the story of Baucis and Philemon, in which two lovers turn into trees. She has difficulty turning the page because she lost the tip of her index finger while cutting trees on the ridge to mark the place where the sun sets. Ada finishes her tale and puts the book away. She decides it is time to turn in for the night and latch the door.

ANALYSIS: SPIRITS OF CROWS, DANCING; EPILOGUE. OCTOBER OF 1874

As winter overshadows "spirits of crows, dancing," death seems to hang suspended over the landscape. The characters are surrounded by a wasteland blanketed in snow. However, warm hearts beat within these frozen surroundings. The icy cabins protect Stobrod and give Ada and Inman some time together. Inman finally seems satisfied, noting that Ada has "filled him full." As in the rest of the novel, in this chapter, it is tempting to read every natural detail as prophetic. Inman notes the absence of a duck he had seen sitting in a lake, but he does not know whether the creature drowned or flew away. Thus, what the duck symbolizes is uncertain. Frazier may be suggesting that there is no way of knowing what will survive and what will perish, since there is no certainty in the world.

This lack of certainty is symbolized most powerfully by Inman's death. Inman is liberated from his anguished life just as he starts to believe in a better future. His death is neither heroic nor gallant, although it is preceded by a thrilling gunfight. Inman is simply shot by Birch, a boy with "empty" eyes and a quick hand. After all the danger and violence that Inman has encountered, it is pathetic that he should be killed so swiftly and unexpectedly. However, there is a measure of peace to his death. As sensory perception fails him, Inman's vision suggests a crossing over to a world of pure spirit. His vision of crows echoes his vision after being shot by the Home Guard in "to live like a gamecock." This bird has been associated with Inman from the novel's very first chapter, "the shadow of a crow"; it seems to capture both the sadness and independence of his spirit. Ada holds her lover as he dies. This moment is the only time in the novel when the narrator withdraws from the action, observing the scene as if from afar. The lovers are allowed one moment alone together.

The epilogue underscores the novel's motif of rotation or the circular passage of time. Ada is shown to draw some comfort from the certainty of seasonal changes that, unlike events in life (and the novel), have neither "inauguration nor epilogue." In spite of great suffering, she seems to have found a measure of peace living with her daughter and Ruby's family at Black Cove. The action of pulling in the "latch-string" suggests a sense of reassurance Ada has gained from a regular routine. Frazier thus ends his novel on a note of equilibrium. The characters experience no more grief, suffering, or upheaval. They simply have followed the turning of the seasons and have embraced the changes that they have encountered.

SUMMARY & ANALYSIS

IMPORTANT QUOTATIONS EXPLAINED

1. Cold Mountain . . . soared in his mind as a place
    where all his scattered forces might gather. Inman did
    not consider himself to be a superstitious person, but
    he did believe that there is a world invisible to us. He
    no longer thought of that world as heaven, nor did he
    still think that we get to go there when we die. Those
    teachings had been burned away. But he could not
    abide by a universe composed only of what he could
    see, especially when it was so frequently foul.

These lines come from the first chapter of the novel, "the shadow of
a crow," in which Inman convalesces in an army hospital before setting out on his epic journey home to Cold Mountain. They suggest
that Inman sees Cold Mountain as a healing place, a spiritual sanctuary where he can retreat from the sufferings of the world. Frazier
shows that Inman has to believe in a world other than the one he
inhabits since his existence itself seems pointless. All that surrounds
Inman is misery, putrefaction, and partition. His sentiments propose that the only way to accept that there is no order to this world
is to know that harmony exists elsewhere. Inman's philosophy is
made more poignant by the fact that his yearning for spiritual
understanding overlaps with his longing to return home. In the
novel, Cold Mountain is both a physical and spiritual place. It is
simultaneously Inman's home and a refuge for his soul.

2. [W]e have against all odds arrived at home, Monroe
    had said. At the time, it was a sentiment Ada took
    with a great deal of skepticism. All of their Charleston
    friends had expressed the opinion that the mountain
    region was a heathenish part of creation . . . Ada's
    informants had claimed the mountaineers to be but
    one step more advanced in their manner of living than
    tribes of vagrant savages.

This passage is from the second chapter of the book, "the ground beneath her hands," and it depicts Ada recalling what her father, Monroe, said the night they first arrived in Cold Mountain. This quote displays the closed mentality of Charleston society—its prejudice, snobbery, and sanctimoniousness. It also shows Ada's initial wariness of the mountain community, a wariness that she later turns towards the "civilized" traits of urban society. It is ironic that the citizens of Charleston, who are presented elsewhere in the novel as proponents of the war, talk about the mountain inhabitants as being "gaunt and brutal," since many of these mountain folk emerge as deeply humane people fighting to survive war's deprivations. However, this quotation shows how a grain of truth may be exaggerated to produce a distorted representation of a group of people—a stereotype. We see the grain of truth in that Inman does meet monstrous people on his journey home, most notably Junior's family; however, we also see the distortion involved in stereotypes in that Inman also meets men and women of great courage and humanity, such as the goat-woman and Sara. This passage displays the ignorance manifest in a closed society, and it suggests the fear inherent in human nature that leads one group of people to demonize another—a tendency that was particularly reflected in North-South hostilities during the Civil War.

QUOTATIONS

3. He had grown so used to seeing death . . . that it
    seemed no longer dark and mysterious. He feared his
    heart had been touched by the fire so often he might
    never make a civilian again.

These lines come in the middle of the novel, from the chapter "to live
like a gamecock," in which Inman barely survives execution at the
hands of Confederate soldiers. For Inman and other soldiers in the
war, death has been demystified because of the war experience, both
on the battlefield and during arduous journeys home. As such, it
stands as a stark indicator of the emptiness of human existence—
suggesting that life is simply a preamble to death—and is a cause for
great despair. This quotation indicates the sheer volume of soldiers
killed in the conflict and how they grow to form a veritable army of
dead men in Inman's mind. This passage follows Inman's resurrection after being shot by the Home Guard, a time when he is most
affected by war's utter wastefulness. Inman's yearning to return
home and resume a normal existence is intensified by his estrangement from the idea of civilian life.

QUOTATIONS

4.   [Ada] believed she would erect towers on the ridge
       marking the south and north points of the sun's
       annual swing. . . . Keeping track of such a thing would
       place a person, would be a way of saying, You are
       here, in this one station, now. It would be an answer
       to the question, Where am I?

As Ada and Ruby lay down roots at Black Cove in the chapter "a satisfied mind," Ada's identification with the natural environment intensifies. Although Inman has yet to return, this quote shows Ada locating herself in nature's cycles, continuing a process of self-realization that provides her with answers to some of life's existential questions. The notion of temporality is key here—Ada begins to think of charting the events of her life as a process in tune with some greater cyclical force. At the end of the novel, we see how this process will frame the events of Ada's life and ultimately ease her sufferings, particularly in the aftermath of Inman's death. Here, Frazier displays his acute sensitivity towards time and place and his characters as beings actively shaped by the forces of nature.

QUOTATIONS

5. But what the wisdom of the ages says is that we do well not to grieve on and on. And those old ones knew a thing or two and had some truth to tell. . . . You're left with only your scars to mark the void. All you can choose to do is go on or not. But if you go on, it's knowing you carry your scars with you.

This passage comes from the chapter "the far side of trouble," when Inman and Ada have been reunited and are hiding out with Ruby and the injured Stobrod at the old "Indian" village. In it, we see a return to the idea of wasted time and of the soul deadened by the evil it has witnessed. Inman admits to feeling ravaged by the war but suggests that his only choice is to move forward in life and to hope to distance himself from its barbarity. Inman recognizes that he has been marked by events but hopes that time will bring a measure of respite. Inman concludes that the most important thing that suffering people can do is to accept the changes they see in themselves, acknowledge the voids within them, and forge ahead. Inman's reference to "those old ones" signifies his identification with the spiritual wisdom of older cultures, particularly the Cherokee.

QUOTATIONS

Key Facts

FULL TITLE
Cold Mountain

AUTHOR
Charles Frazier

TYPE OF WORK
Novel

GENRE
Episodic novel, with a journey structure; romance

LANGUAGE
English, with inclusion of nineteenth-century Southern dialects

TIME AND PLACE WRITTEN
1997, North Carolina, U.S.

DATE OF FIRST PUBLICATION
1997

PUBLISHER
Grove/Atlantic

NARRATOR
Third-person narration, usually according with the perspective of the characters leading the action.

POINT OF VIEW
The novel generally sticks with the protagonists' (Ada's and Inman's) points of view, occasionally shifting to the perspective of other characters.

TONE
Sometimes subdued and reserved, as the characters explore their feelings; often meditative and questioning, as Inman struggles with broader moral or spiritual concerns; occasionally lightly humorous to match characters' good-natured wit.

TENSE
Immediate past

SETTING (TIME)

1864, near the end of the Civil War; the novel refers to events that directy preceded the war and others that occurred decades before.

SETTING (PLACE)

Virginia, before Inman journeys west to North Carolina. Half of the novel is set in the town of Cold Mountain where Ada lives.

PROTAGONIST

The male protagonist is Inman; the female protagonist, Ada.

MAJOR CONFLICT

Both Ada and Inman struggle against the various circumstances—geographical, emotional—that separate them.

RISING ACTION

Inman flees prison and begins journeying toward Cold Mountain; simultaneously, Ada becomes friends with Ruby and learns to survive on her own.

CLIMAX

The major climax occurs when Inman has been shot by Birch, has a vision of dancing crows, and dies in Ada's arms. This event is foreshadowed by Inman's resurrection in "to live like a gamecock" where Inman is buried in a shallow grave and dreams of becoming a crow.

FALLING ACTION

Ruby marries Reid. Ada is living at Black Cove with Ruby's family and her nine year-old daughter, presumably by Inman.

THEMES

Isolation in the search for meaning; knowledge and intuition

MOTIFS

Seasonal changes and rotations; the past

SYMBOLS

The crow; forked roads and crossings; dark-haired women

FORESHADOWING

Many natural events in the novel seem to foreshadow human events; the appearance of the crow often presages death. Inman survives being shot and buried by one team of Home Guard, only to be killed by another set of martial vigilantes.

KEY FACTS

Study Questions & Essay Topics

Study Questions

1. *Discuss why, after all the battlefield carnage that Inman has witnessed, Inman seems to endorse violence on his journey home.*

The slaughter of the battlefield has inured Inman to death, and he has had to draw on his own warrior instincts to survive. Inman thus recognizes that violence is in his blood, but he tries to control when and how he uses it. In addition to biological instincts and concern for survival, both of which emphasize his animalistic side, many different motives compel Inman to fight. Often, as with the incidents involving the three men at the crossroad town, the bear, and the Home Guard at the end of the novel, Inman resorts to violence as a means of self-defense. However, in addition, he sometimes lashes out in righteous anger over other people's culpability. For example, he kills Junior because of his crimes and the three Federal soldiers who stole Sara's hog. Yet Inman endorses more than violence. Inman's decision not to kill Veasey, but to leave him to face the punishment of his own community, shows that Inman is more than just a gun-toting vigilante. Morality is thus not an outdated principle for Inman, even after all the meaningless carnage that he has witnessed. However, he recognizes that war is a feature of the landscape as much as the battlefield. If he has to fight to return home, Inman is willing to do so.

2. *Tales and memories feature prominently in the novel as
    characters frequently call to mind their past lives. Discuss
    why what has previously occurred plays such an
    important role in shaping the novel's plot structure
    and development.*

The novel presents a view of time that is quite abstracted and less
direct then we expect from a work written in the immediate past.
The characters' visions, dreams, memories and folktales cloud over
their present actions, making time seem more of a circular than a linear progression. This ties in with the novel's themes about the cyclical patterns of nature and man's links with the natural world. Ada
and Inman see convergence in the future; the past and present are
simply means of attaining that ultimate goal. Thus, the novel nets
together past and present events to suggest the interweaving of
human lives through time. This theme is made more poignant
because the novel is set in wartime, when memories are often all that
remains of loved ones killed in battle. The ghosts of the past are
recalled so that lost ones are preserved in people's consciousnesses.
Ada and Inman keep each other's pasts alive in their memories to
preserve their hope for the future.

3. *Most of the novel's most dramatic moments turn on the
    theme of freedom and capture. People are trapped,
    hunted, and attacked like animals. Discuss what kind of
    comparison the author is drawing between death in
    nature and killing in the human world.*

Frazier suggests that all men and women are subject to nature's
cycles, and that death is a certainty for every living being. He introduces this theme at the beginning of the novel by quoting Darwin.
The novel suggests that, for one creature to survive, another must
die in order to preserving nature's equilibrium. This equilibrium
encompasses the human world, and so Frazier juxtaposes the con-
flicts in nature with the war between men. Many scenes show characters struggling to gain control over death and to elude the grasp
of its agents, such as the Home Guard, who have the power to
decide who lives and who dies. The author suggests that, in order
to live, men must be free to make their own choices. Inman's freedom of movement is highly restricted; in many ways he is a hunted
man. Similarly, the many slaves within the novel are also leading
oppressed lives. Thus, on different levels, the novel examines
man's fight for liberation and life against the forces of capture,
death, and oppression.

SUGGESTED ESSAY TOPICS

1.   What parallels, if any, does Frazier draw between Ruby and Stobrod's, and Ada and Monroe's relationships? Why are father-daughter relationships so important in the novel?

2.   Inman's experiences at Junior's house are among the novel's most mysterious and unsettling. Why does Frazier present such a savage picture of mountain-dwellers? Doesn't this view of mountain folk seem to support the judgmental views of Charleston society about those who live close to the land?

3.   Despite his distasteful moral code, Solomon Veasey's animation and humorousness make him a particularly human character with whom it is hard not to identify. Why does the author present the preacher in this way, and how does this presentation affect the novel's moral tone?

Review & Resources

Quiz

1. What food does the blind man sell outside Inman's hospital window?

   A. Almonds
   B. Peanuts
   C. Walnuts
   D. Pistachios

2. How does Inman leave the hospital?

   A. He walks through the main door
   B. He jumps off the roof
   C. He steps through a window
   D. He creeps through the basement

3. What song runs through Ada's head after she looks into Esco Swanger's well?

   A. Wayfaring Stranger
   B. Cotton Eyed Joe
   C. Sally Ann
   D. Peas in the Pot

4. What weapon does Inman use to fight off his three attackers at the crossroad settlement?

   A. His rifle
   B. He fights with his fists
   C. Inman threatens them but doesn't use a weapon
   D. A scythe

5.   What is the name of the river Inman crosses in a
     dugout canoe?

     A.   Cape Fear River
     B.   Deep River
     C.   Haw River
     D.   Little River

6.   What possession does Ruby trade for food?

     A.   Stobrod's fiddle
     B.   Ada's cabriolet
     C.   Ada's piano
     D.   Ralph the horse

7.   What precious commodity does Ada find in the
     farmhouse basement?

     A.   Champagne
     B.   Coffee beans
     C.   Tea
     D.   Malt whiskey

8.   Why did Ruby spend a night alone in the woods as a child?

     A.   Her dress was caught on a briar
     B.   She slipped on a root and sprained her ankle
     C.   Night fell and she lost her way
     D.   Stobrod was punishing her

9.   Who or what does Veasey think Inman is when the two first
     meet?

     A.   A vengeful ghost
     B.   A message from God
     C.   The Devil
     D.   A member of the Home Guard

10. Who is Waldo?

     A.   Ada's rooster
     B.   Ada's horse
     C.   Ada's cow
     D.   Ruby's boyfriend

REVIEW & RESOURCES

11. Toward which state is Veasey headed?

    A. Ohio
    B. Texas
    C. Georgia
    D. Tennessee

12. What is the name of the slave girl for whom Odell is searching?

    A. Big Tildy
    B. Abigail
    C. Lucinda
    D. Miranda

13. How does Ruby feel about crows?

    A. She admires them for their wits, resourcefulness, and cunning
    B. She reviles them for their trickery
    C. She likes their black plumage
    D. She is indifferent to them

14. What bird does Ruby claim fathered her?

    A. An eagle
    B. A crow
    C. A flamingo
    D. A heron

15. What European heritage does Ada have?

    A. Her grandmother was Dutch
    B. Her grandmother was Spanish
    C. Her grandfather was French
    D. Her grandfather was German

16. What surprising thing does the slave who looks after Inman following his near-death experience do?

    A. He reads the Bible to him
    B. He draws him a map of the surrounding area
    C. He talks about his own war experiences
    D. He gives Inman a drawing of himself

17. Which Shakespeare play does Ada read out loud to Ruby after they plait each other's hair?

   A.   *Love's Labors Lost*
   B.   *King Lear*
   C.   *Much Ado About Nothing*
   D.   *A Midsummer Night's Dream*

18. According to the Cherokee tale Inman tells Ada, how many days does the Stranger tell the villagers they must fast in order to enter the peaceful world above Shining Rocks?

   A.   Seven
   B.   Fourteen
   C.   One
   D.   Ten

19. What terrible battle does Inman have a recurring nightmare about?

   A.   Malvern Hill
   B.   Petersburg
   C.   Fredericksburg
   D.   Sharpsburg

20. What present does the goat-woman give to Inman when he leaves her camp?

   A.   A drawing of a carrion flower
   B.   A picture of a white goat
   C.   A tract on diet
   D.   A tract on sin and salvation

21. What unusual object does Stobrod put inside the body of his fiddle?

   A.   A snake skull
   B.   A snakeskin
   C.   A snake rattle
   D.   A fang

22. What line from one of Stobrod's songs does Ada write in a letter to Inman?

   A. Return to me is all I ask
   B. I miss you
   C. Come back to me is my request
   D. Please come home

23. What makes the strange musical sound Inman hears by the spring?

   A. Wind chimes
   B. A group of crows cawing
   C. Skeletons hanging in the trees
   D. Pangle playing his banjo

24. What eighth deadly sin does Inman invent to describe his feelings about killing and eating the bear cub?

   A. Woefulness
   B. Despair
   C. Regret
   D. Indigestion

25. What do Ada and Inman propose to do with the old arrow they find stuck in a tree near the Cherokee village?

   A. Return and look at it in the future with their children
   B. Pull it out of the tree and keep it
   C. Take it back with them to show Ruby and Stobrod
   D. Melt the arrowhead down to make matching rings

ANSWER KEY:
1: B; 2: C; 3: A; 4: D; 5: A; 6: C; 7: B; 8: A; 9: B; 10: C; 11: B; 12: C; 13: A; 14: D; 15: C; 16: B; 17: D; 18: A; 19: C; 20: A; 21: C; 22: C; 23: C; 24: C; 25: A

SUGGESTIONS FOR FURTHER READING

BYER, KATHRYN STRIPLING. "On the Trail to *Cold Mountain*." *Shenandoah* 48, no. 1 (1988): 112-117.

GANTT, PATRICIA M., "'Controlling the Image-Making': Domestic Tradition and Women's Identity in Appalachian Literature." *North Carolina Folklore Journal* 42, no. 2 (1995): 91-104.

HOMER, *The Odyssey*. Trans. Robert Fitzgerald. New York: Farrar, Straus and Giroux, Inc., 1998.

KNOKE, PAUL. "Symbolic Artistry in Charles Frazier's *Cold Mountain*." *Notes on Contemporary Literature* 29, no. 2 (1999): 8-10.

MCCARRON, BILL and KNOKE, PAUL. "Images of War and Peace: Parallelism and Antithesis in the Beginning and Ending of *Cold Mountain*." *Mississippi Quarterly* 52, no. 2 (1999): 273-85.

POLK, JAMES. "American Odyssey." *The New York Times*, July 13, 1997, sec. 7.

RUBIN, LOUIS D., JR. et. al., eds. *The History of Southern Literature*. Baton Rouge: Louisiana State University Press, 1985.

REVIEW & RESOURCES